New Directions for
**Adult and Continuing
Education**

Susan Imel
Jovita M. Ross-Gordon
CoEDITORS-IN-CHIEF

Learning Cities for
Adult Learners

Leodis Scott

EDITOR

Number 145 • Spring 2015
Jossey-Bass
San Francisco

LEARNING CITIES FOR ADULT LEARNERS
Leodis Scott (ed.)
New Directions for Adult and Continuing Education, no. 145
Susan Imel, Jovita M. Ross-Gordon, Coeditors-in-Chief

Microfilm copies of issues and articles are available in 16mm and 35mm, as well as microfiche in 105mm, through University Microfilms Inc., 300 North Zeeb Road, Ann Arbor, Michigan 48106-1346.

NEW DIRECTIONS FOR ADULT AND CONTINUING EDUCATION (ISSN 1052-2891, electronic ISSN 1536-0717) is part of The Jossey-Bass Higher and Adult Education Series and is published quarterly by Wiley Subscription Services, Inc., A Wiley Company, at Jossey-Bass, One Montgomery Street, Suite 1200, San Francisco, CA 94104-4594. POSTMASTER: Send address changes to New Directions for Adult and Continuing Education, Jossey-Bass, One Montgomery Street, Suite 1200, San Francisco, CA 94104-4594.

New Directions for Adult and Continuing Education is indexed in CIJE: Current Index to Journals in Education (ERIC); Contents Pages in Education (T&F); ERIC Database (Education Resources Information Center); Higher Education Abstracts (Claremont Graduate University); and Sociological Abstracts (CSA/CIG).

INDIVIDUAL SUBSCRIPTION RATE (in USD): $89 per year US/Can/Mex, $113 rest of world; institutional subscription rate: $335 US, $375 Can/Mex, $409 rest of world. Single copy rate: $29. Electronic only–all regions: $89 individual, $335 institutional; Print & Electronic–US: $98 individual, $402 institutional; Print & Electronic–Canada/Mexico: $98 individual, $442 institutional; Print & Electronic–Rest of World: $122 individual, $476 institutional.

EDITORIAL CORRESPONDENCE should be sent to the Coeditors-in-Chief, Susan Imel, 3076 Woodbine Place, Columbus, Ohio 43202-1341, e-mail: imel.1@osu.edu; or Jovita M. Ross-Gordon, Southwest Texas State University, CLAS Dept., 601 University Drive, San Marcos, TX 78666.

Cover design: Wiley
Cover Images: © Lava 4 images | Shutterstock

www.josseybass.com

CONTENTS

EDITOR'S NOTES   1
Leodis Scott

1. Evolution and Reconstruction of Learning Cities for   5
Sustainable Actions
Connie Watson, Aimee Tiu Wu
A discussion of learning cities requires social sustainable change that
traces its roots back to the idea of a "learning society," which featured
a lifelong education movement long before the common expression of
lifelong learning.

2. Learning Cities, Systems Change, and Community   21
Engagement Scholarship
Hiram E. Fitzgerald, Renee Zientek
Community engagement scholarship describes the mutual relationship in
higher education for civic, community, and public engagement that create
systems for service learning in the context of a learning city/region.

3. Workplace, Organizational, and Societal: Three Domains of   35
Learning for 21st-Century Cities
Lyle Yorks, Jody Barto
Interconnections between workplace and organizational learning inform
how learning cities and regions must function to promote learning for a
larger society.

4. Public Libraries and Cooperative Extension as Community   45
Partners for Lifelong Learning and Learning Cities
Alysia Peich, Cynthia Needles Fletcher
Public libraries, land-grant institutions, and Cooperative Extension are
just a few existing examples in America concerned with adult education
serving the larger adult learner community.

5. A Connected History of Health and Education: Learning   57
Together Toward a Better City
Joanne Howard, Diane Howard, Ebbin Dotson
Health and education must be included in any strategic planning of learn-
ing cities; such implications must consider how to improve the social
quality of life for children and adults.

6. Role of Leisure in Humanizing Learning Cities   73
Dan K. Hibbler, Leodis Scott
Leisure shares a special connection with adult education from ancient
times to significant events in history such as the Industrial Revolution;
these connections play a part in the need for leisure education that is essential for social and human development.

7. Learning Cities for All: Directions to a New Adult Education   83
and Learning Movement
Leodis Scott
Through encouraging leadership from the adult and continuing education
field, the idea of learning cities can be realized and implemented within
existing communities across America.

INDEX   95

EDITOR'S NOTES

Adult education needs more space. It has certainly outgrown its current domain, given all the varieties, diversities, and complexities of learning. We scholars and practitioners must start building larger spaces for all learners. This volume suggests that adult and continuing educators begin building "learning cities" to take the lead in our continued commitment to lifelong learning and education. Beyond the traditional walls of schools, colleges, and workplaces, learning cities will be constructed for all life experiences, attaching to common issues that are often unnoticed within individuals, families, communities, and societies.

From the start, it may seem odd to claim that cities can learn. Attributing human qualities to seemingly lifeless objects appears out of place, especially with a prior understanding that learning can only occur within individuals. Still, there is a need to account for how people, as citizens, collectively can act to bring about change on a broad societal scale. Therefore, I'm suggesting that large communities and metropolitan areas (such as cities) can take on the characteristics of learning through unified actions that broaden their spaces for more inclusion. The purpose of *Learning Cities for Adult Learners* is to show not only the possible ways that cities can learn, but also to describe how adults (irrespective of social class or educational level) may experience a new quality of life.

As such, the chapter authors write from their informed perspectives in promoting the idea of learning cities and, hopefully in some small measure, start to further remove old divisions of town and gown, the ivory tower against the real world, academic and corporate knowledge sharing, and even adult–continuing education versus vocational–technical training. Instead, the idea of learning cities promotes the development of learning, education, and engagement in its entirety. For all these reasons, this volume looks for practices that expand the traditional limited spaces that currently exist and encourages a more widespread approach to educate and learn across disciplines, within communities, and inside the minds of all people.

Chapter 1 considers the evolution and reconstruction of learning cities to sustain continued actions of improvement. Connie Watson and Aimee Tiu Wu describe how learning cities evolved from the historical discussion of the "learning society" and how broader perspectives of "learning communities" must consider the environmental, health, economic, and social aspects. These authors start the recurrent theme in this volume of the important differences between the theories of lifelong learning and lifelong education within the concept of learning cities.

Systems change and community engagement scholarship offer an evidence-based practice framework that can anchor learning cities/regions in data-driven decision making. In Chapter 2, Hiram E. Fitzgerald and Renee

NEW DIRECTIONS FOR ADULT AND CONTINUING EDUCATION, no. 145, Spring 2015 © 2015 Wiley Periodicals, Inc.
Published online in Wiley Online Library (wileyonlinelibrary.com) • DOI: 10.1002/ace.20118

Zientek review recent developments in the literature on learning cities and present their recent work on the landscape of engaged scholarship and a strategy of learning cities as a system.

In Chapter 3, there is a focus on how learning cities might be considered in the organizational learning context. Lyle Yorks and Jody Barto explore workplace learning, organizational learning, and societal learning as three domains in the 21st century, viewing learning cities as larger organizations for learning.

Alysia Peich and Cynthia Needles Fletcher in Chapter 4 explain how public libraries are excellent examples of existing lifelong learning structures that learning cities can adopt, and also how the history of land-grant institutions and cooperative extensions can be further advanced. In Chapter 5, Joanne Howard, Diane Howard, and Ebbin Dotson provide an important contribution from the perspective of public health and the social contract of America on how learning cities can address the overall quality of life, health, and education, thus improving schools and health care.

In Chapter 6, Dan K. Hibbler and I explore how leisure scholars and adult learning educators can work together to also improve the quality of life through a comprehensive leisure education, exposing false dichotomies and traditional views about leisure and work. In the concluding chapter, I make a final comment about learning cities from an American perspective that attempts to advance further philosophical, theoretical, and practical discussions in the adult and continuing education field. This chapter provides a conceptual framework of learning cities in the context of existing theories and practices within the field.

It should be noted that the discussion in this volume about learning cities may be somewhat different from previous conceptualizations on the topic. During the earlier stages of preparing this volume, I remember talking to a professional in urban planning, who embraced the learning cities idea and started to think about how to construct buildings and create citywide transportation to promote learning. In other words, his view was that a learning city would have, in both form and function, an urban design so that all citizens would experience what learning is, live in a space built for learning, and travel in an environment inspiring others to learn.

Although at that time I never thought about the mechanical changes a learning city could take, it has now heightened my overall awareness in the construction of learning cities. To think about the architectural design of a city along with creating a plan that captures all learning experiences could advance this idea in substantial ways. For example, consider where you live now: What would it take to change your environment into a learning city? How would parks, libraries, and museums change, or what would be the new appearance of local schools, colleges, and universities? Even though talking with the urban planner has sparked such questions about future structural changes, in the meantime, everyone can change his or her mindset about the construction of education and learning. Working together, learning cities may do more than expand the space of adult education; they may transform the mentality of the whole world.

Over 40 years ago, in a 1972 UNESCO publication entitled *Learning to Be: The World of Education Today and Tomorrow*, Edgar Faure and his colleagues introduced visions for "lifelong education for all" by presenting 21 recommendations in reforming education around the world. The Faure Report (Faure et al., 1972) argued for expanding the *domain* of education that would include all people, irrespective of age or social status. It envisioned education entering into its true domain that exists beyond systems, schools, universities, or other static edifices and toward expansive functions of learning. As the Faure Report explained:

> If we admit that education is and will be more and more a primordial need for each individual, then not only must we develop, enrich and multiply the school and the university, we must also transcend it by broadening the educational function to dimensions of society as a whole. (pp. 161–162)

Thus, the most important reform by the Faure Report is that education exists in all sectors of society, especially within cities. It suggested that the city contains "immense educational potential" because of its social and administrative structures, cultural networks, vitality of exchanges, as well as constituting a "school for civic sentiment and fellow-feeling" (Faure et al., 1972, p. 162).

Any discussion of learning cities in a new context of America must consider the intentions of the Faure Report and other related terms. For example, there is a momentous shift in communication from the expression of lifelong *education* for all (as expressed in the Faure Report) to a newer expression of lifelong *learning* for the individual. Wain (2000) further explained this change about lifelong education being replaced with lifelong learning as education "abandonment" for a neutral form of learning. The Faure Report vision promoted lifelong education "as the master concept for educational policies," thus concluding, "Lifelong education, in the full sense of the term, means that business, industrial and agricultural firms will have extensive educational functions" (p. 198).

In these ways, the development of a learning city invigorates the lifelong education movement that considers the educational functions of an entire society, where the *academy* serves its society in the same way that Ernest Boyer (1997) described, as a "more vigorous partner in the search for answers to our most pressing social, civic, economic, and moral problems" (pp. 81–82).

The learning city, in essence, would engage all sectors and people in society as *partners* confronting our common problems, issues, and concerns—the same way that Longworth (1999) concluded, "A learning city is one with plans and strategies to encourage wealth-creation personal growth and social cohesion through the development of the human potential of all its citizens and working partnerships between all its organizations" (p. 187).

New Directions for Adult and Continuing Education • DOI: 10.1002/ace

This volume intends to add thoughts and ideas to inform any such plan of actions for learning cities, now and in the future. Such intentions call for the field of adult and continuing education to move to a new space that leads toward a movement in constructing learning cities for all.

Leodis Scott
Editor

References

Boyer, E. L. (1997). The scholarship of engagement. In E. L. Boyer (Ed.), *Ernest L. Boyer: Selected speeches 1979–1995* (pp. 81–92). Princeton, NJ: Carnegie Foundation for the Advancement of Teaching.

Faure, E., Herrera, F., Kaddoura, A., Lopes, H., Petrovsky, A., Rahnema, M., & Ward, F. R. (1972). *Learning to be: The world of education today and tomorrow* (Faure Report). Paris, France: UNESCO.

Longworth, N. (1999). *Making lifelong learning work: Learning cities for a learning century.* Sterling, VA: Kogan Page.

Wain, K. (2000). *The learning society in a postmodern world: The education crisis.* New York, NY: Peter Lang.

LEODIS SCOTT *is a cofounder and research scholar at LearnLong Institute for Education and Learning Research, and lecturer in adult learning philosophy and practice at DePaul University–School for New Learning and Columbia University–Teachers College.*

1

This chapter describes how the concept of learning cities evolved from the "learning society" and the lifelong education and learning movements, and advances multiple forms of communities of learning.

Evolution and Reconstruction of Learning Cities for Sustainable Actions

Connie Watson, Aimee Tiu Wu

Introduction

Philosophers, religious leaders, poets, and citizens from a variety of cultures have shaped many ideals found in the modern description of a learning city, which includes solving practical community problems in a sustainable way for individuals and communities (Juceviciene, 2010). More recently, the idea of the learning society, with learning for the promotion of social change at its core, has been used as a framework to help guide individuals and communities as they navigate the global society (Jarvis, 2007). This chapter will explore the evolution of the learning city, including how it has been influenced by the learning society, lifelong education, and lifelong learning literature. It will also briefly provide a historical overview of the learning city movement—including its reconstruction—contemplate implications for adult educators, and make recommendations for future research.

Evolution of the Learning City

Key ideas that support the learning city concept have come from a variety of cultures and are connected to early thinkers and leaders. For example, Plato noted that the main goal of education was to empower citizens to contribute to the social fabric of the community and live in peace and harmony (Longworth & Osborne, 2010). In addition, Eastern ideas like the "Confucian wisdom [of] ... living harmoniously, becoming an undivided 'I' with the universe" had long inspired great thinkers and leaders to create a truly harmonized society (Sun, 2007, p. 97). Longworth and Osborne (2010) further described many ancient cities (e.g., Venice, Istanbul, Jerusalem, and Damascus) that embraced a strong link between prosperity, cultural enlightenment, and learning. The learning society, as a more recent concept, has been used to describe the

NEW DIRECTIONS FOR ADULT AND CONTINUING EDUCATION, no. 145, Spring 2015 © 2015 Wiley Periodicals, Inc.
Published online in Wiley Online Library (wileyonlinelibrary.com) • DOI: 10.1002/ace.20119

connection between education, learning, prosperity, and civic engagement (Jarvis, 2007). This section will briefly describe the learning society starting with two movements that informed this concept: lifelong education and lifelong learning. Next, connections between these ideologies and that of the learning city will be explored.

Lifelong Education, Lifelong Learning, and Learning Society. Lifelong education has roots in the writings of Basil Yeaxlee and Eduard Lindeman from the mid-1920s where they promoted the ideas of reflection on experience, reform of all educational providers, holistic education, educating throughout life, self-directed learning, and vocational/nonvocational education (Smith, 1996/2001). Lifelong education embodies the idea that learning continues throughout life and through this process people increase their competence (knowledge, skills, and abilities) and thus have more control over their environment (Iqbal, 2009). Early conceptualization of lifelong education combined pedagogy and andragogy, and focused on formal and informal education through workplace learning, distance education, continuing education, and correspondence courses (Iqbal, 2009). Furthermore, Freirean philosophy and pedagogy were closely aligned to the lifelong education movement. The aim of Freire was to bring about a better world through emancipatory education, active citizenship, praxis (reflection) and conscientization, and critical awareness of one's social reality (Freire, 2000; Jackson, 2007). However, Freire also pointed to the political structure of education on a deeper level and believed that "teaching . . . can never be divorced from critical analysis of how society works, and teachers must challenge learners to think critically about the social, political, and historical realities within which they inhabit the world" (Jackson, 2007, p. 203). Therefore, lifelong education embraced a variety of key principles including educational reform, informal and formal learning, the intersection of politics and hegemony, the educational systems, personal reflection, and conscientization. This wide focus and "the vagueness of the notion and its capacity to be used to serve very different political ends has opened [lifelong education] up to considerable critique" (Smith, 1996/2001, para. 10).

Later in the 1960s and 1970s, UNESCO took up the lifelong education movement as an organizing principle and a number of authors from various countries (e.g., Faure, Illich, Reimer, Freire, Holt, and others) promoted its importance for the betterment of society (Boshier, 2005; Smith, 1996/2001). For example, in "Learning to Be," lifelong education was promised as a master concept for reform of entire education systems (Faure et al., 1972). This suggested that a "proper application of lifelong education would result in the creation of a learning society where access to and learning in education would be taken for granted—an inalienable human right like clean water or a roof over one's head" (Boshier, 2005, p. 373). It was proposed that this type of learning society would support the seamless movement from formal to informal learning throughout the lifespan, and policies and resources from the government and business organizations would support equal and continual access to and funding of education, as well as fostering an appreciation for education in all sectors of society (Boshier, 2005; Smith, 1996/2001).

Lifelong learning, as compared to lifelong education, has been described as less emancipatory, with less obligation on educators to address social conditions and more support of capitalism, and is "nested in vocationalism" (Boshier, 2005, p. 375). This ideology is seen by some as an oppressive shift from governments and power structures (as the defenders and providers of education) to the people being responsible for their own education and learning. Because "if the learner as consumer does not take advantage of available opportunities it is their own fault . . . it is easier to blame the victim than overcome structural or psychological barriers to learning" (Boshier, 2005, p. 375).

On the other hand, lifelong learning has also been viewed as a positive force where governments and ruling parties give over ownership of education and learning to the masses (Boshier, 2005). For example, the Organization for Economic Co-operation and Development (OECD) described lifelong learning from a socioeconomic perspective in its 2007 report, *Qualification Systems: Bridges to Lifelong Learning*, which takes on a broader perspective of lifelong learning than a primarily economic focus of the 1970s (OECD, 2007). The OECD (2007) report promotes a four-pronged approach to lifelong learning: systemic view, centrality of the learner, motivation to learn, and multiple objectives of education policy. However, due to the economic focus of this international organization, it is not surprising that the impetus to support lifelong learning from the OECD perspective is the positive relationship between the goals of educational attainment and economic growth (OECD, 2007). Furthermore, the responsibility to be educated is given to the individual; as OECD states, the aim is to "improve knowledge and competencies for all individuals who wish to participate in learning activities" (p. 10). However, the report also acknowledges that governments, businesses, and educational institutions need to provide systems and structures that support lifelong learning and thus this conceptualization does not completely divorce power structures from their responsibility of supporting and promoting lifelong learning.

Currently, lifelong learning is considered the predominant ideology describing lifelong formal and informal education (Boshier, 2005). As noted in the OECD (2007) report, lifelong learning has adopted a broader perspective of ongoing education that includes economic, political, religious, psychosocial, and historical perspectives and has an ultimate goal of individual and social growth and development (Iqbal, 2009). Consequently, the more emancipatory focus on learning and the call for reform directed by the lifelong education movement is no longer at the forefront of this discourse (Boshier, 2005).

Both lifelong education and lifelong learning literature made connections to the learning society. These movements were said to support the creation of a learning society. In the 1990s, the learning society began to be described, debated, and discussed as an ultimate goal of lifelong formal and informal education and learning (Jarvis, 2007). A number of authors supported the idea that rapid social change at the local and global level in response to advancing technologies and the increasing interconnectedness of people, ecosystems, and economies within and across borders are the major impetus for developing a learning society in the 21st century (Hamilton & Jordan, 2010; Longworth & Osborne, 2010; Su, 2010). Furthermore, these changes are moving the global society from an industrial to a knowledge-based economy where continuous learning is the fuel that drives and sustains the local and global cultures (Su, 2010). As society shifts and changes, individuals and societies need to be able to question their own assumptions and cultural metanarratives so that people and communities can successfully adapt and lead (Su, 2010). It may be that a learning society fosters the mental agility needed to contemplate and act within supercomplex environments through the use of reflective learning (Kegan, 1982; Su, 2010).

Jarvis (2007), a major thinker on the concept of learning society, described it as "one in which the majority of social institutions make provisions for individuals to acquire knowledge, skills, attitudes, values, emotions, beliefs and senses within a global society" (p. 100). Jarvis pointed out that learning takes place at the individual level while noting that society can support learning through encouraging policies, structures, and norms. However, Jarvis (2007) also clarified that transformation can take place at the social level but the responsibility lies with the individual. This ideology focuses on learning as opposed to education and assumes that individuals have enough social power or social capital to influence change and make an impact.

Alternately, Sun (2007) described how the learning society is analogous to the harmonious society and while he acknowledged that individuals "are the essence of society" (p. 97), he differs in his conceptualization from Jarvis (2007) by emphasizing social construction. Sun (2007) attests that the harmonious society is "also a critical reflection on Chinese tradition, which values harmony and characterizes human social values and moral responsibilities for healthy and positive relationships of human beings with nature, society, and self" (p. 97). Therefore, the learning society is described as a process and an outcome where the mutually beneficial process of lifelong learning supports the development of this type of society.

Interestingly, learning cities and other closely aligned movements (learning regions, towns, villages, and/or festivals) incorporate some of the lifelong education and lifelong learning foci including the importance of educating individuals throughout their lives in formal and informal ways (Boshier, 2005; Faure et al., 1972; OECD, 2007). "A learning city (town or village) is a form of community development in which local people from every community sector act together to enhance the social, economic, cultural and environmental conditions of their community. It is a pragmatic approach that mobilizes the learning resources and expertise of all five community sectors," namely, government, business, nonprofit, education, and citizens and community groups (Boshier, 2005, p. 377).

In these ways, the learning city takes the emancipatory and utopian ideologies of lifelong education and marries them with the economically driven and vocationally focused lifelong learning movement; at the same time, the learning city embraces the development of a global learning society by implementing practical, contextual, and sustainable solutions within targeted cities and regions.

Trends, Initiatives, and Milestones of the Learning City Movement. In a comprehensive study of historical precedents and current trends in learning communities, Longworth and Osborne (2010) detailed the growth of the learning city and region beginning with the foundational initiative called "Educating Cities" spearheaded in the 1970s by the OECD. The seven cities from original member states tapped to organize educational strategies in lifelong learning included Edmonton (Canada), Gothenburg (Sweden), Vienna (Austria), Edinburgh (Scotland), Kakegawa (Japan), Adelaide (Australia), and Pittsburgh (United States). This movement began to gain massive momentum in the 1990s with the launching of the International Association of Educating Cities based in Barcelona (Spain). Today, the association has a 400-city membership spanning from Europe, North America, Australia, and Japan. In addition, the mid-1990s witnessed the great contributions by the now defunct European Lifelong Learning Initiative (ELLI) and World Initiative on Lifelong Learning (WILL). Their collective messages and policies of lifelong learning and learning cities were adapted by some learning regions during the early years of the organization. In 1996, Liverpool became the pioneer "City of Learning" in Europe followed by other cities in the United Kingdom like Southampton, Norwich, Edinburgh, Birmingham, and others. In recognition of the potential socioeconomic contributions to society, other European cities like Espoo, Gothenburg, and Dublin quickly followed suit (Longworth & Osborne, 2010).

Another milestone during this period was the development of the *Learning Cities Audit Tool* (EUROlocal, 2014; Longworth & Osborne, 2010), an interactive questionnaire with 10 indicators: commitment to a learning city; information and communication; partnerships and resources; leadership development; social inclusion; environment and citizenship; technology and networks; wealth creation, employment, and employability; mobilization, participation, and the personal development of citizens; and learning events and family involvement. The purpose of this tool was to assess member cities' understanding of the concept of learning cities, its implications, and how lifelong learning can be supported in their respective cities. The results from this audit confirmed uncertainty and ambiguity about the frameworks of learning city/region and lifelong learning in general, but also elicited strong interest from many major European municipalities. This in turn prompted the development of a major policy paper by the European Commission and became the motivation for other countries like Finland, Czech Republic, Italy, Ireland, France, Germany, and Norway to join the learning cities movement (EUROlocal, 2014; Longworth & Osborne, 2010).

In 2001, OECD undertook a substantial learning regions project resulting in a book called *Cities and Regions in the New Learning Economy*, detailing the economic benefits of developing a learning region and transformation of cities and its citizens. Informed by the robust contributions in Europe, ideas and policies about learning communities/regions started to spread across the world. For example, Australia initiated a small-scale audit in 10 communities to strategize learning cities and elevate it to national level. The State of Victoria emerged as a key player in the Australian experience and led in the development of a key document outlining its vision as a learning region within the local, national, and global context with the aim of promoting not only economic growth, but also social inclusion and good governance. Other initiatives (e.g., "learning festivals" in Adelaide) started to take place in other parts of Australia but were unfortunately short-lived. In 2002, Germany initiated a national project called the Länder into 71 "learning regions" with the goal of spurring economic development through educational overhaul by spreading the necessity for cultivating lifelong learning across the region (Longworth & Osborne, 2010; OECD, 2001).

Since 2003, the European Commission funded a number of projects with the intention of stimulating interest in learning regions. Noteworthy were the LILLIPUT and PALLACE (promoting active lifelong learning in Australia, China, Canada, and Europe) projects. LILLIPUT, a set of 14 web-based modules, focused on the different aspects (e.g., historical, educational, cultural, economic) of the construction of a learning society, while PALLACE, a more comprehensive resource, linked the global partners across the seven learning regions around the world—South-East Queensland, South Australia; Auckland, New Zealand; CEFEL in France; The Learning Region in Espoo, Finland; The Edmonton Region in Canada; Beijing, China; and Edinburgh, Scotland (Longworth & Osborne, 2010; PASCAL International Observatory, 2014).

As learning regions spread across the world, Europe remained pragmatically focused on the indicators of success and effectiveness. Learning audits like LILARA Project (Learning in Local and Regional Authorities) became a trend in assessing learner needs and suggested recommendations for local and regional educational providers. Today, a global initiative is headed by PASCAL International Observatory (Place and Social Capital and Learning), a global partnership among policy makers, researchers, analysts, higher education, NGOs, and the private sector. PASCAL's main role is to support and strategize the design and implementation of learning regions within the framework of each geography, city, and district (PASCAL International Observatory, 2014). Currently, the PURE project (PASCAL Universities in Regional Engagement) under PASCAL supports member regions with research into the role of university systems in the development and promotion of regional, social, economic, cultural, and environmental development. In conjunction with PASCAL, PENR3L (PASCAL European Network of Regions of Lifelong Learning) developed the *Limerick Declaration* detailing strategic directions and recommendations to help promote sustainable learning regions. Unwavering in its commitment to the development and promotion of learning regions, the European Commission since 2009 has funded EUROlocal, a centralized repository of resources obtained from PENR3L. With a wealth of web-based resources aimed at helping member regions disseminate knowledge, it is hoped that this will allow for sharing of best practices relevant to a learning region among educational providers like universities, private sectors, local and regional government agencies, cultural institutions, and NGOs (EACEA, 2009; EUROlocal, 2014; Longworth & Osborne, 2010; PASCAL International Observatory, 2014).

Reconstruction of the Learning City: A Vision of Next Actions

As our society flourishes on the foundation of its ever-expanding knowledge economy accelerated by significant advances in information and communication technologies, mounting concerns are emerging about our contemporary ways of living (Laszlo & Laszlo, 2007). Today, we have become accustomed to a lifestyle of tremendous energy consumption with irreversible environmental destruction.

In reconstructing a truly sustainable learning city, we initially refer to what Juceviciene (2010) cites as seven principles from other works: stability and vitality of the system, environmental sustainability, economic sustainability, social sustainability, cultural sustainability, educational sustainability, and international issues of sustainability. The overarching goal of which is to "creat[e] a simpler and more meaningful way of producing what we need in order to reestablish the balance between our human systems, the biosphere, and the geosphere in which they rest" (Laszlo & Laszlo, 2007, p. 501). An example of a learning city practicing sustainable development is Kaunas (second largest city in Lithuania), where the brainchild of *Strategy for Kaunas as a Learning City* was created based on praxis as a result of empirical research, SWOT analysis, and the decisions of the Learning City Council (Juceviciene, 2010). In addition, Kearns (2012) supplies other principles for building sustainable learning cities that include developing a shared vision, building partnership, addressing social justice and equity, involving the community actively, progressing learning in many contexts and forms, making development strategic, and addressing the big issues confronting cities (Kearns, 2012, p. 373).

Learning communities are instrumental in addressing key social and economic issues such as preserving the environment, eradicating poverty, promoting healthy living, personal development, and social cohesion while working toward attaining economic prosperity (Kearns, 2012). But the foremost challenge toward sustainability facing cities and regions worldwide is the increasing rural and international migration, which Wood and Landry (2008) coined as "the central dilemma of the age" (p. 23). To leverage on the synergy of diversity, stakeholders might consider journeying to "the intersection" or the "Medici effect," where diverse and even differing ideas converge to form path-breaking innovations to produce value-added outcomes and enhance multisectoral/multicultural collaborations (Johansson, 2004, as cited in Kearns, 2012).

Implications and Actions for Adult Education

What strengths and expertise do we adult educators have that might help us ignite a learning cities movement in the United States? In partial answer to this query, we come from a wide range of backgrounds, work in multiple social sectors, have strong research and assessment skills, and carry a passion to use education/learning as tools to promote positive change in our communities. There is strength in our diversity along with a common language and focus to our field.

Partnership Building. As adult educators, entrusted with promoting the message and value of lifelong learning, we play a vital role in promoting the mutual interests of economic prosperity, human development, social–environmental sustainability, and deepening partnerships across all sectors of the society (Laszlo & Laszlo, 2007). Learning communities represent a commitment to locate learning at the core of the city/region through strategic partnerships (Faris, 2008). In working toward a sustainable learning city/ community/region/society, extending partnerships among stakeholders and building a shared vision of the future are key (Kearns, 2012). The humble seeds planted in the development and implementation of learning cities have the potential to sow sustainable, harmonious, and healthy communities.

Assessment. To determine continued funding and program success, individual and organizational learning with its research and assessment must continue to emerge with a strong focus on learning outcomes. As Maki (2004) notes, "assessment becomes an institution's means to examine its educational intentions on its own terms within the complex ways that humans learn and within the populations an institution serves" (p. 15). Similar to school assessment, we find relevance and compatibility in Hipp and Huffman's (2007) suggestion of utilizing assessment tools as "frames to stimulate conversations related to creating and sustaining PLCs (Professional Learning Communities)" (p. 119).

Assessment of learning cities/regions is especially difficult because the students are diverse and widespread (all ages, found within many different institutions and organizations, also represent multiple ethnicities and cultures) and the goals are connected to organizational learning and social change. Evaluating the effectiveness of learning city initiatives to solve local problems (job loss, poverty, environmental decline) and improve social conditions (education, healthy, happiness, and peace) is difficult and complex. However, this does not mean we as adult educators should shy away from the challenge. It may be that we need to utilize participatory action research and other qualitative research designs, in addition to the quantitative methods already being administered, to more deeply understand the impact of learning city programs and initiatives.

New Directions for Adult and Continuing Education • DOI: 10.1002/ace

Role of Adult Educators: Opportunity for Dialogue in the United States. While this chapter provides a glimpse of the complex framework of learning cities, we wish to highlight the importance of the role of adult educators in promoting lifelong learning, revitalizing the concept of learning communities, and sustaining efforts across multisectors. Similar to Marsick, Bitterman, and van der Veen (2000), we recommend mentoring, advising, experiential learning, and creating an open and welcoming learning environment where learners can engage in reflexive dialogue. As in the case of Scotland, where the University of Glasgow played a central role in developing and coordinating the Pascal International Observatory and the Learning Cities 2020 initiative, as adult educators we have an opportunity to continue this dialogue in the United States. In general, adult educators have the educational background, expertise, and experience necessary to take the lead in establishing a forum where citizens from multiple sectors of society can come together and discuss, apply, and research learning city philosophy and practice. It is interesting that the learning city movement has not been as prominent in the United States, especially given the problems at the city/state/regional levels in relation to educational reform, unemployment, discrimination, poverty, health care, and other sociocultural, political, and economic issues. Therefore, this type of interdisciplinary, community-based movement may be able to promote cooperation and spur national action.

Additional Considerations for Reconstructing Learning Cities

As previously mentioned, there is an opportunity for adult educators to continue the dialogue and action involved in reconstructing learning cities in the context of the United States. The PASCAL International Observatory, with its *Learning Cities 2020* initiative and *Learning Cities Networks* (PASCAL International Observatory, 2014), provides an agenda that can be advanced that considers the limitations inherent in the learning city movement. Such advancement can lead to an actionable agenda, which can be supported, evaluated, and revised through integrated governance and partnerships supporting learning city goals and initiatives. Research, particularly action research and adult education, may be implemented in a three-pronged approach that considers limitations and challenges of learning cities, sustainable actions of economic growth and social harmony, and integrated partnership between local, national, and global agencies, including public and private education systems.

Challenges and Limitations of Learning Cities. First of all, future research should more deeply investigate the limitations and challenges in regard to developing and promoting a learning city/region. Similar to the learning society ideal, the learning city philosophy, which is influenced by this ideal as well as by lifelong education and lifelong learning, has idealistic goals that may never be able to come to fruition (Hughes & Malcolm, 1995). Furthermore, learning communities and societies "come and go depending on historical shifts in power. They are not linear developments in the creation of critical, moral, and democratic societies" (Alexander, 2006, p. 595). Therefore, questions surrounding the ideals of the learning city and its realistic implementation given the zeitgeist of the times should be genuinely investigated.

Secondly, future research should deconstruct the several challenges inherent in the practical implementation of the learning city. For example, Osborne, Kearns, and Yang (2013) described a list of challenges including rapid urbanization, mass migration into cities, environmental challenges, human rights issues, growing economic inequality between citizens, and loss of shared community and identity of community members. Any one of these challenges could be the foci of future research based on pre- and postevaluations surrounding a learning city intervention.

In particular, future research could discern the level of uneven distribution of education and learning programs associated with a learning city. This is partially due to the fact that the affluent often have increased access to learning resources, networks, and events (Wang, Song, & Kang, 2006). For example, many cities, regions, and nations have implemented TED Talks (Technology, Entertainment, and Design Talks) such as TEDxPhiladelphia (http://tedxphiladelphia.org/) where speakers with innovative and creative ideas share their thoughts with the public. These conferences and events may cost money and individuals have to be connected to the association to have access and obtain tickets to participate. Therefore, an individual's political network and socioeconomic status may often dictate what educational and learning resources are available. Any city/region can actually have a vibrant learning city for the upper and middle class while at the same time have inadequate learning and education resources available to those in poverty and/or marginalized. More research is needed to uncover the systems, norms, and psychosocial conditions promoting these discrepancies.

Sustainable Actions of Economic Growth and Social Harmony. Besides researching the limitations and challenges found within the learning city movement, different types of collaborative, participatory, and action learning research should be utilized when implementing and evaluating learning city initiatives. For example, action learning "builds learning environments around collaborative work on real problems" (O'Neil & Marsick, 2007, p. xviii). In this way, practical action can be taken in cities/regions to help solve problems and improve living and learning conditions while at the same time insight and learning can be acquired in a systematic way to find out how and if the implementation strategies were effective on an individual and/or social level. Four areas to consider when conducting action research in the learning city include a focus on green cities, healthy cities, economically strong cities, and socially resilient and robust cities (Alexander, 2006; Kearns, 2012; Layard, 2005; Osborne et al., 2013).

Green cities focus on environmental supports and improvements within the city and/or region. They often work to balance the three pillars of sustainable development—social, economic, and environmental. Kearns (2012) described green cities as "EcCoWell" cities where the economy, community, and well-being of its citizens are the major intertwined goals of the region (p. 368). Next, healthy cities encompass the physical and social environments in relation to individual and community health. The World Health Organization has embraced this ideology with a focus on the following healthy city goals: reducing health inequalities (Mackenbach & Bakker, 2002), supporting maternal and children's health (Wilkinson & Marmot, 2003), and linking good health to optimal social functioning (Petersen & Lupton, 1996).

Third, economically strong learning cities are part of the focus of almost all learning city themes found in the literature. As noted earlier, the OECD supports this focus; however, other authors warn of the problems associated with a purely economic bent to the implementation of a learning city (OECD, 2007). However, that could be said of any learning city initiative that didn't have a holistic approach. Besides concentrating on prosperity, job creation, and vocational skill building, the economic approach may also support a creative bent. For example, UNESCO in 2004 started the Creative Cities network. This approach links economic development to the growth of culture and community in cities. The idea is that creative cities promote the local creative industries found in the community, and this spurs economic growth and increases creation, production, and consumption of cultural goods and services and understanding of the diversity found within the local culture (UNESCO, 2013).

Lastly, learning cities with a social perspective at the heart of their initiatives are concerned with individual and community happiness, harmony, peace, and social justice (Alexander, 2006; Layard, 2005; Sun, 2007). For example, Layard (2005) in *Happiness* describes an "evidence-based vision of how we can live better" (p. ix) by focusing on individual and community happiness. Although Layard did not state that his ideas are connected to the learning city approach, his premise described that supportive social structures such as strong community health, the promotion of work–life balance, sustainable development and economies, decreases in inequality, strong family and community relationships and values, and personal freedom are connected to happiness.

More recently, Layard collaborated with the Earth Institute, Columbia University, and edited the *World Happiness Report* along with Helliwell and Sachs (Helliwell, Layard, & Sachs, 2012). This report integrates all four perspectives noted above (social, economic, green, and healthy) and calls for action. "[I]f we act wisely, we can protect the Earth while raising quality of life. ... We can do this by adopting lifestyles and technologies that improve happiness ... while reducing human damage to the environment" (Helliwell et al., 2012, p. 3). The authors go on to elucidate the connection between building happy communities and sustainable development making the point that a balanced society is more apt to be a lasting and thriving one—for there are many ills associated with affluence and inequity (e.g., climate change, obesity, anxiety, and violence). Although these authors do not use the terms learning society or city, there is much similarity in their proposed approach for social sustainable change with the literature described in this chapter, including a philosophical/spiritual dimension. "Aristotle and the Buddha advised humanity to follow a middle path between asceticism on the one side and craving material goods on the other" (Helliwell et al., 2012, p. 4). A complete comparative analysis is outside the scope of this chapter but further research investigating the connections between the *World Happiness Report* and the learning cities movement could illuminate important findings and highlight innovative and practical applications that support both lines of inquiry.

Research may be conducted on one or more of these areas that describe cities. This can depend on the goals and context of the learning city/region and the research objectives for understanding, creating, applying, and reporting these initiatives.

Integrated Partnership Between Local, National, and Global Systems. These four areas describing cities as green, healthy, economic, and social may complement or distract from one another depending on the focus and implementation strategy of the learning city. Therefore, future research should not only investigate the limitations and challenges connected to learning cities and contemplate the different kinds of learning cities including their effectiveness, but should also focus on the systems and structures that support and challenge a learning city approach. One example of how a learning city initiative can be fostered through a connection between governments, educational systems, and business and industry is the Goldman Sachs 10,000 Small Businesses Initiative (Goldman Sachs, 2014). Goldman Sachs as a major international business has partnered with Babson University to provide entrepreneurial education and training to local small businesses. Goldman Sachs and Babson University partner with each city's government, community organizations, and work with a local community college to roll out the free program. This initiative has been implemented in 10 cities, as of 2014, including New York, Philadelphia, Chicago, and Detroit (Goldman Sachs, 2014). Therefore, research identifying how successful such initiatives are, as well as how these partnerships are created and maintained, would certainly provide useful information that could be applied to new enterprises. Furthermore, it will be important to research what systems and structures help keep programs like these viable and operational over the long term.

Lastly, in 2013, the MacArthur Foundation unveiled the Cities of Learning initiative (MacArthur Foundation, 2014). This strategy links youth to learning opportunities throughout the city and online. The youth then track their learning using digital badges and can provide access to these learning portfolios to schools, employers, and other organizations. The Cities of Learning initiative presents "open badges" by stating "Badges help make [skills, achievements, and interests] count towards your education, career and lifelong learning" (MacArthur Foundation, 2014).

Chicago was the first city to launch this program and now has over 100 organizations assisting over 100,000 students with their learning journeys. The key strategy supporting the program is connected learning, which includes key learning principles (interest powered, peer-supported, and academically oriented) with design principles (openly networked, production-centered, and a shared purpose). Other cities involved in this movement include Los Angeles, Dallas, Columbus, Pittsburgh, and Washington DC. The Cities of Learning initiative and the Goldman Sachs 10,000 Small Businesses are just two examples of a number of innovative initiatives taking place across the United States and the globe.

The challenge for adult educators is to integrate these initiatives into a collaborative and focused Learning Cities approach so that the energy, innovation, and expertise around these seemingly individual movements can be leveraged to reduce redundancy, share resources, and cooperate around a common goal. The difficulty will be in figuring out how to make connections while still providing autonomy so that processes stay organic and creative but ultimately work together not in opposition. We must start by raising awareness to all that is already begun, then dialogue about what could be done, and lastly find common ground where we can work together to create the type of learning cities that will be vibrant, sustainable, and healthy for many generations to come.

References

Alexander, D. (2006). Beyond a learning society? It is all to be done again: Zambia and Zimbabwe. *International Journal of Lifelong Education*, 25(6), 595–608.

Boshier, R. (2005). Lifelong learning. In L. M. English (Ed.), *International encyclopedia of adult education* (pp. 373–378). New York, NY: Macmillan Publishers.

EACEA. (2009). Lifelong learning programme: Key activity 4—Dissemination and exploitation or results. Brussels, Belgium: Education, Audiovisual & Culture Executive Agency. Retrieved from http://eacea.ec.europa.eu/llp/results_projects/documents/c09ka4_en.pdf

EUROlocal. (2014). *LILARA learning needs audit tool for learning city administration employees*. Retrieved from http://pobs.cc/5rn6

Faris, R. (2008). *Learning communities: Cities, towns and villages preparing for a 21st century knowledge-based economy*. Report submitted to the Resort Municipality of Whistler and the Centre for Curriculum, Transfer and Technology, Victoria. Retrieved from http://members.shaw.ca/rfaris/LC.htm

Faure, E., Herrera, F., Kaddoura, A., Lopes, H., Petrovsky, A., Rahnema, M., & Ward, F. (1972). *Learning to be: The world of education today and tomorrow*. Paris, France: UNESCO.

Freire, P. (2000). *Pedagogy of the oppressed*. New York, NY: The Continuum International Publishing Group.

Goldman Sachs. (2014). *10,000 small businesses*. Retrieved from http://www.goldmansachs.com/citizenship/10000-small-businesses/US/

Hamilton, R., & Jordan, L. (2010, June). *Learning cities: The United Kingdom experience*. Heritage, Regional Development and Social Cohesion International Conference, Ostersund, Sweden.

Helliwell, J., Layard, R., & Sachs, J. (Eds.). (2012). *World happiness report*. New York, NY: The Earth Institute, Columbia University.

Hipp, K. K., & Huffman, J. B. (2007). Using assessment tools as frames for dialogue to create and sustain professional learning communities. In L. Stoll & K. S. Louis (Eds.),

Professional learning communities: Divergence, depth and dilemmas (pp. 119–131). New York, NY: Open Press University.

Hughes, C., & Malcolm, T. (1995). The myth of the learning society. *British Journal of Educational Studies, 43*(3), 290–304.

Iqbal, M. J. (2009). Lifelong education: A conceptual debate. *International Journal of Media, Technology and Lifelong Education, 5*(1). Retrieved from http://seminar.net/index.php /volume-5-issue-1-2009-previousissuesmeny-126/117-life-long-education-a-conceptual -debate

Jackson, S. (2007). Freire re-viewed. *Educational Theory, 57*(2), 199–213.

Jarvis, P. (2007). *Globalization, lifelong learning and the learning society: Lifelong learning and the learning society* (Vol. 2). New York, NY: Routledge.

Johansson, F. (2004). *The Medici effect: Breakthrough insights at the intersection of ideas, concepts and cultures.* Boston, MA: Harvard Business School Press.

Juceviciene, P. (2010). Sustainable development of the learning city. *European Journal of Education, 45*(3), 419–436.

Kearns, P. (2012). Learning cities as healthy green cities: Building sustainable opportunity cities. *Australian Journal of Adult Learning, 52*(2), 368–391.

Kegan, R. (1982). *The evolving self: Problem and process in human development.* Cambridge, MA: Harvard University Press.

Laszlo, K., & Laszlo, A. (2007). Fostering a sustainable learning society through knowledge-based development. *Systems Research and Behavioral Science, 24*(5), 493–503.

Layard, R. (2005). *Happiness: Lessons from a new science.* New York, NY: Penguin Press.

Longworth, N., & Osborne, M. (2010). Six ages towards a learning region: A retrospective. *European Journal of Education, 45*(3), 368–401.

MacArthur Foundation. (2014). *Cities of learning.* Retrieved from http://citiesoflearning.org

Mackenbach, J., & Bakker, M. (2002). *Reducing inequalities in health: A European perspective.* London, UK: Routledge.

Maki, P. L. (2004). *Assessing for learning: Building a sustainable commitment across the institution.* Sterling, VA: Stylus.

Marsick, V., Bitterman, J., & van der Veen, R. (2000). *From the learning organization to learning communities: Toward a learning society.* Retrieved from ERIC database. (ED440294)

OECD. (2001). *Cities and regions in the new learning economy.* Retrieved from http:// learningcities2020.org/sites/default/files/pdfs/OECD-Cities_in_Learning_Econ.pdf

OECD. (2007). *Qualification systems: Bridges to lifelong learning.* Retrieved from http://www .oecd.org/education/innovation-education/38465471.pdf

O'Neil, J., & Marsick, V. J. (2007). *Understanding action learning.* New York, NY: American Management Association.

Osborne, M., Kearns, P., & Yang, J. (2013). Learning cities: Developing inclusive, prosperous and sustainable urban communities. *International Review of Education, 59,* 409–423.

PASCAL International Observatory. (2014). *Learning Cities 2020.* Retrieved from http:// pascalobservatory.org/

Petersen, A., & Lupton, D. (1996). *The new public health: Health and self in the age of risk.* London, UK: Sage.

Smith, M. K. (1996/2001). *Lifelong learning, the encyclopedia of informal education.* Retrieved from http://www.infed.org/encyclopaedia.htm

Su, Y. (2010). The learning society: Two justifications. *Australian Journal of Adult Learning, 50*(1), 10–25.

Sun, Q. (2007). A critical view on building learning cities in China: Lifelong learning as a vehicle towards a harmonious society. *Convergence, 40,* 95–116.

UNESCO. (2013). *Creative cities network mission statement.* Retrieved from http://www .unesco.org/new/fileadmin/MULTIMEDIA/HQ/CLT/pdf/Mission_statement_Bologna_cr eative_cities_meeting.pdf

Wang, A., Song, G., & Kang, F. (2006). Promoting a lifelong learning society in China: The attempts by Tsinghua University. *Higher Education Management and Policy, 18*(2), 1–16.

Wilkinson, R., & Marmot, M. (2003). *Social determinants of health: The solid facts* (2nd ed.). Copenhagen, Denmark: The Regional Office for Europe for the World Health Organization.

Wood, P., & Landry, C. (2008). *The intercultural city: Planning for diversity advantage.* London, UK: Earthscan.

CONNIE WATSON is an assistant professor of psychology at the Community College of Philadelphia, cofounder and research scholar at LearnLong Institute for Education and Learning Research, and lecturer for the Goldman Sachs 10,000 Small Businesses Initiative–Philadelphia.

AIMEE TIU WU is a cofounder and research scholar at LearnLong Institute for Education and Learning Research.

2

Learning cities/regions, as education systems, require the practice frame-work of community engagement scholarship that anchors systems change for data-driven decision making.

Learning Cities, Systems Change, and Community Engagement Scholarship

Hiram E. Fitzgerald, Renee Zientek

During the latter part of the 20th century, a zeitgeist enveloped vast segments of society drawing education, business, civil society, and government toward similar conclusions with respect to approaches to problem solving. During most of the century, the prevalent approach to problem solving was to fund specific projects designed to produce evidence-based practices, which then could be taken to scale beyond the initial demonstration context. In too many cases, such efforts failed to produce desired system-wide transformative change. Gradually, change agents began to realize that project-focused efforts to produce change were too often disconnected from the broader systems within which projects were embedded. Change efforts began to shift to more directly focus on changing systems as well as the specific problems embedded within those systems. The development of learning cities/regions (LCRs) is one such effort. However, a focus on systems change does not mean that targeted interventions seeking effective practices should be abandoned. Rather, outcomes or data produced by project-focused change efforts are valuable and should provide input to more systemic models which then can guide structured or data-driven decision making.

In this chapter we argue that community engagement scholarship (CES) is an evidence-based practice framework that can anchor LCR systems change efforts to data-driven decision making. In addition, we suggest that service learning provides a framework for structuring lifelong or transformational learning, a core component of the LCR approach to economic development and quality of life. First, we provide a brief context for these propositions by summarizing the core principles of LCRs as we understand them. Second, we trace the emergence of CES as an approach focused on program- and system-level change achieved through scholarship-focused university–community partnerships. We especially draw attention to the affordances provided by a comparison of CES and LCRs with respect to efforts to promote systems

NEW DIRECTIONS FOR ADULT AND CONTINUING EDUCATION, no. 145, Spring 2015 © 2015 Wiley Periodicals, Inc.
Published online in Wiley Online Library (wileyonlinelibrary.com) • DOI: 10.1002/ace.20120

change, economic development, lifelong learning, and innovation and creativity for 21st-century knowledge societies and economies. Third, we draw particular attention to the role of service learning as a framework for generating lifelong learning opportunities for individuals and organizations, drawing on commonalities between service learning and transformational learning (Mezirow, 1997, 2012; Pinzon & Arceo, 2006; Stage & Wells, 2014). We conclude with recommendations for building even stronger interconnections among the four helixes believed to be important for achieving sustainable systems change: higher education, business, government, and civil society (Cooper, 2011).

Learning Cities/Regions (LCRs)

The concept of a learning city has its origins in reports advanced by the Organization for Economic Co-operation and Development (OECD, 2002) in the latter part of the 20th century. A learning city was envisioned as a city where all segments of society shared a commitment to "promote inclusive learning from basic to higher education, revitalize learning in families and communities, facilitate learning for and in the workplace, extend the use of modern learning technologies, enhance quality and excellence in learning, and foster a culture of learning throughout life" (UNESCO Institute for Lifelong Learning, 2014, p. 27). Clearly, the LCR effort is one designed to transform systems where innovation, learning, and economic development flourish at all levels of the life span.

The OECD (2002) report identified two interconnected learning domains, individual and organizational, where lifelong learning can provide an expansion of knowledge capacity. Each domain is essential for the systems change LCRs seek to achieve. Individual learning refers to knowledge acquisition, knowledge transfer, and knowledge creation with heavy emphasis on active learning and implicit involvement of indigenous or tacit knowledge in the creation process. Individual learning from LCR and transformative learning perspectives are conceptualized as occurring across the lifespan from infancy through adulthood, with particular emphasis on continued learning during the adult years.

Organizational learning occurs within institutional contexts focusing on knowledge production and application, such as business firms, research and development institutes, innovation centers, and smart zones. In order to stimulate system-level transformations, such organizations need to build networks of partnership collaborations in which each partner can grow its enterprise while simultaneously aligning with the system-wide goals and objectives that benefit all. "Networking and partnerships are key ingredients, since collective learning and robustness depend on a continuous exchange and flow of information about products, processes and work organization. The links happen usually between organizations, which have a long-standing relationship based on stability and trust, but also between towns, cities and regions themselves" (OECD, 2002, p. 8). Interactions among organizations in a network are shaped by institutions and their unique structures, practices, routines, and modes of relating to others. Critical to systems change, organizations need to be committed to practices built upon principles of dynamic, nonlinear open systems, emphasizing forecasting models, scenario planning, and data-driven decision making rather than rules and routines that threaten innovation and create impermeable boundaries that stifle competitiveness. In short, efforts to effect systems change must be driven by pragmatism, critical realism, and relativism as philosophies of science (Bechara & Van de Ven, 2007); linear cause–effect positivist approaches simply are not adequate to assess dynamic open systems change.

Participants at the UNESCO-sponsored Institute for Lifelong Learning Beijing International Conference on Lifelong Learning agreed to 12 practices designed to advance the LCR agenda (UNESCO Institute for Lifelong Learning, 2014, pp. 24–27):

1. Empowering individuals and promoting social cohesion
2. Enhancing economic development and cultural prosperity
3. Promoting sustainable development
4. Promoting inclusive learning in the education system
5. Revitalizing learning in families and communities
6. Facilitating learning for and in the workplace
7. Extending the use of modern learning technologies
8. Enhancing quality in learning
9. Fostering a culture of learning throughout life
10. Strengthening political will and commitment
11. Improving governance and participation of all stakeholders
12. Boosting resource mobilization and utilization

If implemented, their commitments promise exciting transformational changes for cities and regions around the world. However, from a CES perspective, there is a critical element missing from the list of 12. That element is embodied in one of the core defining features of CES, namely, its emphasis on outcome evaluation. Do innovations lead to outcomes that provide evidence of sustainability? Does implementation of lifelong learning have the desired effect of promoting equity and social justice? Do lifelong learning initiatives lead to decisions that enhance the quality of life for all citizens in a particular culture? The list of questions is likely endless, but what is common to all of them is that the answers can only be guided by outcomes, and outcomes are linked to the multiple approaches for obtaining tacit and explicit data (Nonaka & Takeuchi, 1995), and then testing whether the outcomes generated by efforts to change a system or a portion of a system radiate throughout the system or transfer to other systems. The multiple forms of

Table 2.1. Commonalities and Differences in Key Aspects of Community Engagement Scholarship (CES) and Learning Cities/Regions (LCRs)

CES	LCRs
Life span	Life span
Evidence-based	Place-based
Authentic partnerships	Individual and organization learning
Systems change (systems focus)	Systems change (economic focus)
Education	Education
Government	Government
Business	Business
Civil society	Civil society
Sustainability	Sustainability
Systems change models	Systems and networks formation
Cocreation of knowledge	
Data-driven decision making	
Collective impact metrics	
Focus on scholarship	
Discovery: new knowledge	
Application: scaling up	
Learning	Learning
Dissemination (outreach)	Dissemination (outreach)
Innovation	Innovation
Democratization of knowledge	Democratization of knowledge
Equity and social justice	Equity and social justice

scholarship-driven inquiry embedded within higher education institutions (HEIs) form the knowledge value that HEIs can bring to LCR partnerships. Table 2.1 illustrates similarities and differences in LCR and CES approaches to systems change and problem solving. Note the striking similarities and the heavy emphasis in CES on evidence generation and assessment. Figure 2.1 illustrates traditional efforts made to find solutions to systems of complex problems, sometimes also called wicked problems or what Ackoff (1999) called messes (see Alpaslan & Mitroff, 2011). For example, a common solution to problems related to K–12 education is to enhance the skill levels of teachers. However, singular programmatic efforts are likely to produce little change if change processes do not also involve government (funding for training programs), business (truly perceiving K–12 education as workforce development and investing in it), and civil society (stronger parental involvement in local K–12 educational change efforts, such as increasing neighborhood safety). Finally, all segments of the helixes of systems change have to focus on the collective impact of multiple program projects so that the system is affected, not just the target object of the initial intervention. Moreover, change efforts must be innovative, risk-worthy, sustainable, knowledge-driven, evidence-based, entrepreneurial, and anchored in education (Figure 2.2).

New Directions for Adult and Continuing Education • DOI: 10.1002/ace

Figure 2.1. Conceptual Framework for Linking Efforts to Solve Complex Problems Through Individual Projects With System-Wide Change Initiatives Focused on Collective Impact

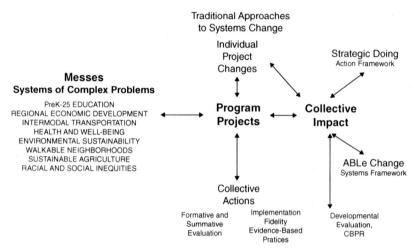

Systems Change, Program Projects, Collective Impact, and Evidence-Based Practice

Figure 2.2. Illustration of the Interconnectedness of Four Helixes of Systems Change and Seven Key Characteristics of Community Engagement Scholarship

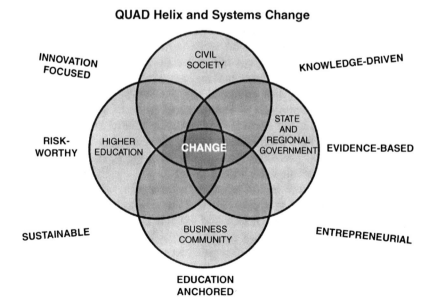

QUAD Helix and Systems Change

Community Engagement Scholarship (CES)

During the last quarter of the 20th century, higher education was challenged to reconnect with society and contribute to the resolution of a broad range of societal problems. Commissions (Kellogg Commission, 2001), visioning retreats (Brukardt, Holland, Percy, & Zimpher, 2004), professional organizations (Bruns, 2010; Goettel & Haft, 2010), definitions (Fitzgerald, Smith, Book, Rodin, & CIC Committee on Engagement, 2005), and white papers (Fitzgerald, Bruns, Sonka, Furco, & Swanson, 2012) were created in response to the challenges, and higher education's response was robust. Many policies and practices were enacted to facilitate development of university–community partnerships and to address societal problems through community-based research and evaluation, service learning and civic engagement, recognition of the value of tacit knowledge, and efforts aimed at the democratization of knowledge.

CES focuses on the development of evidence-based partnerships between HEIs and community partners that attempt to solve an explicit problem or tackle complex or wicked problems through blended knowledge and cocreative efforts (Fitzgerald, 2014; Fitzgerald & Simon, 2012). The concept of LCRs embraces a commitment to lifelong learning that is inclusive of individuals and organizations located within a place-based system in order to create vibrant, innovative, and economically successful communities and enhanced quality of life for all (Longworth & Osborne, 2010; OECD, 2002; Osborne, Kearns, & Yang, 2013). CES focuses on evidence-based systems analysis, which may or may not be place-based, at least in a localized sense.

CES recognizes that cocreative and blended knowledge collaborations with community partners increase the asset base that can inform efforts designed to reduce barriers to transformative change through evidence-based practices. Investigators in HEIs who work with communities soon realize that blended knowledge optimizes the bidirectional transfer of knowledge and facilitates data-driven decision making, asset-based change models, and evidence-based practices, and enhances the plausibility of producing sustainable change. This approach to learning and problem solving is consistent with community-based participatory research (CBPR) approaches used in university–community partnerships where the goal is to seek solutions to community-defined problems through the blending of explicit and tacit knowledge (Nonaka & Takeuchi, 1995).

Efforts to find partial or full solutions to complex, wicked messes are more effectively anchored in approaches that are informed by everyday politics and a genuine flow between tacit and explicit knowledge and a broader set of methodological approaches to guide data-driven structured decision making. Moreover, such approaches require everyone to understand that the component parts of dynamic open systems are never static. Because perturbations in open systems produce changes that are nonlinear, dynamic, and relativistic, structured decision making about systems change must be an ongoing process.

Today's challenge is to build upon the historical research successes of higher education while seeking contemporary solutions to such problem areas as renewable and green energy, quality of air and water, educational equity, talent development, access to food, sustainable agriculture, advanced manufacturing, birth to higher education, and health and well-being. CES emphasizes implementation of change models using community-based research approaches, systems frameworks, and systems modeling with the goal of enhancing and sustaining equity and justice within and between cities and regions. Moreover, CES recognizes that input from all four helixes of systems change must be represented in development of the change models being developed, implemented, and evaluated for their effectiveness.

Why focus on cities and regions? The answer is remarkably simple: the majority of humanity now resides in an urban area. Moreover, urban areas generate nearly all jobs and consume the largest percentage of all of society's services and needs. Population demographers and social critics increasingly draw attention to the inequitable distribution of wealth that supports disparities within and between societies with disproportionate concentration in densely populated urban contexts. In their thorough analysis of the pervasive impact of inequity, Wilkinson and Pikett (2009) note that "Inequality is associated with lower life expectancy, higher rates of infant mortality, shorter height, poor self-reported health, low birth weight, AIDS and depression" (p. 81). Their analysis of economic disparities convincingly documents that the quality of life for everyone is directly related to reduction in the disparities of resources across all sectors.

Cities and regions with concentrated poverty, weak social ties, and poor-to-no economic base do not have the financial capital to sustain efforts at transformational change. Often they are perceived as not having the social or human capital to effect, implement, and sustain change as well. One reason for this perception is that many power brokers and key decision makers do not incorporate indigenous or tacit knowledge into the planning process. Devaluing or ignoring community knowledge and basing decisions on outside preferences often produces efforts to change communities that ultimately are not sustainable because the voices of civil society were not part of the proposed change process. Efforts to meaningfully change complex systems have historically been based on quick-fix interventions rather than long-term critical analysis of the systemic factors that render program–project change efforts ineffective (McNall et al., in press; also see Figure 2.1). The relationship networks individuals and organizations create are influenced by social–cultural norms and practices, which in turn produce interconnected networks and increasingly complex systems of information exchange. To understand and to attempt to effect transformational change, therefore, require change agents to understand systems as interdependent and nonlinear entities. Such understandings are informed by the blended flow of tacit and explicit approaches to knowledge, and the combined wisdom from all four helixes involved in systems change. Without such understandings and efforts to incorporate tacit knowledge in change efforts, it is extremely difficult to build trust among individuals or organizations.

CES brings this framework to the local, regional, and global levels (Fitzgerald & Simon, 2012) with its emphasis on shared knowledge, cocreated solutions, and action-oriented systems change efforts. Because HEIs can be neutral connectors within the quad-helix system, they are uniquely positioned to guide discussions to data-driven decision making, evidence-based practices, and incorporation of community voices at all levels of the process.

According to the editors of the recently published Global University Network for Innovation's book *Knowledge, Engagement & Higher Education: Contributing to Social Change*, "An intelligent society must be ready to generate knowledge corresponding with transnational knowledge societies and networks. The idea of an intelligent society recognizes that all human beings have the capacity to create knowledge in the context of creating a new way of living or a new society" (Escrigas, Sanchez, Hall, & Tandon, 2014, p. xxxiv). Higher education's commitment to CES can be the driving force that ensures that the pathways taken to ensure equity, justice, and regeneration of society are guided by blended tacit and explicit knowledge data-driven decision making, evidence-based practices, and the collective impact of partnership networks spanning the quad helix of systems change. Indeed, understanding that knowledge has multiple sources and is created inside as well as outside the university requires a new framework for conceptualizing knowledge and building collaborative partnerships across all sectors of society. Moreover, such efforts must be driven by a problem-solving approach that involves what Boyte (2004) refers to as "everyday politics." Everyday politics are in action when ordinary citizens mobilize to tackle everyday problems. According to Peters and Eatman (2014), "Everyday politics of this sort reflects a view of politics as an activity people engage in when they work together across lines of difference to advance their interests and values. The practice of this kind of politics including naming and framing common problems; expressing and examining values, interests, and desired ends and goals; considering what can and should be done to address common problems and pursue interests and ends; building an exercising power; and acting together in ways that involve reconciliation and negotiation over different and often conflicting values, worldviews, interests and ends" (pp. 173–174). In short, systems change is hard and complicated work! It requires opportunities to have experience in multiple contexts and recognizes the important role that civil society can play in addressing community problems, most of which have lifelong impacts.

Service Learning

Service learning is an established form of CES within the context of Boyer's (1996) concept of the scholarship of engagement (see also Glass & Fitzgerald,

2010). The New England Resource Center for Higher Education (NERCHE, 2014) defines engaged scholarship as follows:

> The term redefines faculty scholarly work from application of academic expertise to community engaged scholarship that involves the faculty member in a reciprocal partnership with the community, is interdisciplinary, and integrates faculty roles of teaching, research, and service. While there is variation in current terminology (public scholarship, scholarship of engagement, community-engaged scholarship), engaged scholarship is defined by the collaboration between academics and individuals outside the academy—knowledge professionals and the lay public (local, regional/state, national, global)—for the mutually beneficial exchange of knowledge and resources in a context of partnership and reciprocity. The scholarship of engagement includes explicitly democratic dimensions of encouraging the participation of non-academics in ways that enhance and broaden engagement and deliberation about major social issues inside and outside the university. It seeks to facilitate a more active and engaged democracy by bringing affected publics into problem-solving work in ways that advance the public good with and not merely for the public. (NERCHE, 2014, para. 1)

In service learning, teaching is organized around sharing knowledge with various audiences in formal or informal settings. The teaching is based on relationships and the learning context (Doberneck, Glass, & Schweitzer, 2010). While service learning is commonly associated with formal credit-bearing activities that link service with learning objectives through reflection, the concepts of service learning can be adapted and embedded in many other learning settings ranging from community education to professional and talent development for individual learners as well as organizations and networks. Service learning is an ideal approach for addressing community problems involving the environment, economy, education, and health.

In service learning, the learner gains a better understanding of the subject through his or her service/engagement and in the critical reflection on his or her experience. There is real potential for all involved in service learning to play the role of both teacher and learner. The reciprocity involved in service learning creates a diverse community of experts. Those experts, when combined, hold a vast knowledge of the community and have diverse perspectives on how to tackle even the most complex community problems. In service learning, students, faculty, staff, partner organizations, and community members are all contributors to knowledge and all have the potential to both teach and to learn.

Service learning is about relationships. It is about the relationship between the learner and the teacher and about the relationship between what's learned and how it is applied to real problems through service and engagement. When relationships with community organizations are strong, students (learners) are more likely to benefit from meaningful, high-caliber projects. Reciprocal, long-term, and sustainable relationships can emerge—relationships in which students gain knowledge, skills, and professional networks. Agencies benefit from added capacity, increased information, technical knowledge, and contributing to development of future employees. To paraphrase Taleb (2010), faculty achieve a greater understanding of community organizations (Littlepage & Gazley, 2013) by having repeated opportunities to realize that "what you don't know [is] far more relevant than what you do know" (p. xxiii). Unknowns may include issues related to the local political system in which community agencies may be embedded, variations among community organization board members with respect to unit mission, and the fragility of community office holders who are part of the elected officials initially involved in a project but are subject to constituent pressures. Recognizing that faculty may have few, if any, opportunities to experience these situations in their everyday academic work is an important consideration. Service learning, for the student, the faculty member, and the community partner, is anchored in the same philosophies that characterize CES: pragmatism, critical reflection, and relativism.

Lifelong Learning and Lifelong Engagement: An Essential Combination. Whereas service learning is a pedagogy that promotes lifelong engagement and the responsibilities of being a member of a community, the concept of lifelong engagement takes a different shape when considering adult learners and non-college-bound youth, among other populations. Adult learners and non-college-bound youth are not always involved in formal learning settings such as a classroom. Nevertheless, institutions of higher education can facilitate the learning and engagement of such individuals through service learning and other forms of community-engaged scholarship.

When considering the contributions that all members of communities may make toward the health and vitality of a city, region, and country, one must consider how lifelong engagement is connected to lifelong learning. The concept of being a lifelong learner is essential to the concept and formation of LCRs. In building a culture of teaching and learning that supports learning cities, it is critical to establish a culture of lifelong *engagement* because its long-term outcomes are not only anchored in the production of a needed workforce, but also in the revitalization of older workers to meet workforce needs created by innovation and change in the workplace. Lifelong engagement creates a generative cycle for innovation and captures tacit and explicit knowledge, creating an environment/network for the transfer of knowledge. It is a rejection of unidirectional banker education (Freire, 1970/2012) and an affirmation of colearning and cocreation of knowledge through self-reflection (also see Mezirow, 1997, 2012).

Active, public citizenship begins with and is grounded in our everyday institutional environments—the places where we live and work, go to school, volunteer, and participate in communities of faith. It is public-spirited and practical, not utopian or immaculate, but part of the messy, difficult, give-and-take process of problem solving (Boyte, 1995); that is, it involves everyday politics.

Conclusions and Recommendations

In this chapter, we have illustrated that the similarities between two approaches to systems change far outweigh their differences. LCRs attempt to transform cities or regions by focusing on learning as a comprehensive life-long experience across all sectors of society. CES attempts to draw together the same sectors but around models of change that can be linked to benchmarks and metrics that can be used to guide the change process. We offered the well-established practices of service learning and civic engagement, which connect individuals and community partners (organizations) in experiential learning activities to their mutual benefit, as one model for structuring life-long learning in LCRs. Each of these approaches to effect transformational change shares commitments to authentic partnership building; development of local capacity for learning, innovation, and change; enhancement of educational opportunities across the life span; inclusiveness and social justice; creating vibrant centers for economic growth and development; and advancing art and culture.

In order to bring these commitments into reality, agents from all four helixes of systems change need to (a) build stronger support for the development of HEI–community partnerships; (b) draw upon both tacit and explicit knowledge in efforts to solve complex problems; (c) invest in emergent or developmental evaluation as a fundamental aspect of all systems change efforts; (d) strive to eliminate social–economic and racial inequities; (e) develop programs that provide expanded opportunities for all age groups to engage in service and learning community settings as both teachers and learners and, most of all, as equal problem solvers; and (f) emphasize data-driven decision making consistent with one of the declarations formed by the participants at the 2013 Beijing Declaration on Building Learning Cities who committed to envisioning "that a learning city will facilitate individual empowerment, build social cohesion, nurture active citizenship, promote economic and cultural prosperity, and lay the foundation for sustainable development" (UNESCO Institute for Lifelong Learning, 2014, p. 24). We envision that HEIs united through CES with their partners in civil society, business, and government can stimulate development of LCRs and truly create knowledge-based places where emergent knowledge blends with acquired wisdom that yields commitment to lifelong learning throughout society.

References

Ackoff, R. L. (1999). *Re-creating the corporation*. New York, NY: Oxford University Press.

Alpaslan, C. M., & Mitroff, I. I. (2011). *Swans, swine, and swindlers: Coping with the growing threat of mega-crises and mega messes*. Stanford, CA: Stanford University Press.

Bechara, J. P., & Van de Ven, A. H. (2007). Philosophy of science and engaged scholarship. In A. H. Van de Ven (Ed.), *Engaged scholarship: A guide for organizational social research* (pp. 36–70). Oxford, UK: Oxford University Press.

Boyer, E. (1996). The scholarship of engagement. *Journal of Public Service and Outreach, 1*, 11–20.

Boyte, H. (1995). *Reinventing citizenship: The practice of public work.* Minneapolis: University of Minnesota, Humphrey Institute of Public Affairs.

Boyte, H. (2004). *Everyday politics: Reconnecting citizens and public life.* Philadelphia: University of Pennsylvania Press.

Brukardt, M. J., Holland, B., Percy, S. L., & Zimpher, N. (2004). *Calling the question: Is higher education ready to commit to community engagement.* Milwaukee Idea Office, University of Wisconsin-Milwaukee, Milwaukee.

Bruns, K. S. (2010). Small partnership leads into National Outreach Scholarship Conference. In H. E. Fitzgerald, S. Seifer, & C. Burack (Eds.), *Engaged scholarship: Contemporary landscapes, future directions: Vol. 2. Community–campus partnerships* (pp. 349–360). East Lansing: Michigan State University Press.

Cooper, D. (2011). *The university in development: Case studies of use-oriented research.* Cape Town, South Africa: Human Services Research Council.

Doberneck, D. M., Glass, C. R., & Schweitzer, J. H. (2010). From rhetoric to reality: A typology of publicly engaged scholarship. *Journal of Higher Education Outreach and Engagement, 14*(5), 5–35.

Escrigas, C., Sanchez, J. G., Hall, B., & Tandon, R. (Eds.). (2014). *Knowledge, engagement & higher education: Contributing to social change.* London, UK: Palgrave Macmillan.

Fitzgerald, H. E. (2014). Knowledge, engagement and higher education in the United States and Canada. In C. Escrigas, J. G. Sanchez, B. Hall, & R. Tandon (Eds.), *Higher Education in the World 5: Knowledge, engagement & higher education: Rethinking social responsibility* (pp. 227–244). New York, NY: Palgrave Macmillan.

Fitzgerald, H. E., Bruns, K., Sonka, S. T., Furco, A., & Swanson, L. (2012). Centrality of engagement in higher education. *Journal of Higher Education Outreach and Engagement, 16*(3), 7–27.

Fitzgerald, H. E., & Simon, L. A. K. (2012). The world grant ideal and engagement scholarship. *Journal of Higher Education Outreach and Engagement, 16*(3), 33–55.

Fitzgerald, H. E., Smith, P., Book, P., Rodin, K., & CIC Committee on Engagement. (2005). *Draft CIC report: Resource guide and recommendations for defining and benchmarking engagement.* Champaign, IL: Committee on Institutional Cooperation.

Freire, P. (1970/2012). *Pedagogy of the oppressed.* New York, NY: Bloomsbury.

Glass, C. R., & Fitzgerald, H. E. (2010). Engaged scholarship: Historical roots, contemporary challenges. In H. E. Fitzgerald, C. Burack, & S. Siefer (Eds.), *Handbook on engaged scholarship: Contemporary landscapes, future directions: Vol. 1. Institutional change* (pp. 9–24). East Lansing: Michigan State University Press.

Goettel, R., & Haft, J. (2010). Imagining America: Engaged scholarship in the arts, humanities and design. In H. E. Fitzgerald, S. Seifer, & C. Burack (Eds.), *Engaged scholarship: Contemporary landscapes, future directions: Vol. 2. Community–campus partnerships* (pp. 361–373). East Lansing: Michigan State University Press.

Kellogg Commission. (2001). *Returning to our roots: Executive summaries of the reports of the Kellogg Commission on the Future of State and Land-Grant Universities.* Washington, DC: National Association of State Universities and Land Grant Colleges.

Littlepage, L., & Gazley, B. (2013). Examining service learning from the perspective of community organization capacity. In P. H. Clayton, R. G. Bringle, & J. A. Hatcher (Eds.), *Research on service learning: 2B Communities, institutions, and partnerships* (pp. 419–440). Sterling, VA: Stylus.

Longworth, N., & Osborne, M. (2010). Six ages toward a learning region: A retrospective. *European Journal of Education, 45*, 368–401.

McNall, M. A., Brown, R. E., Barnes-Najor, J. V., Doberneck, D., Fitzgerald, H. E., & Springer, N. C. (in press). Systemic engagement: Universities as partners in systemic approaches to community change. *Journal of Higher Education Outreach and Engagement.*

Mezirow, J. (1997, summer). Transformative learning: Theory to practice. In P. Cranton (Ed.), *New Directions for Adult and Continuing Education: No. 74. Transformative learning in action: Insights from practice* (pp. 5–12). San Francisco, CA: Jossey-Bass.

Mezirow, J. (2012). Learning to think like an adult: Core concepts of transformative theory. In E. W. Taylor & P. Cranton (Eds.), *The handbook of transformative learning: Theory, research and practice* (pp. 73–95). San Francisco, CA: Wiley.

New England Resource Center for Higher Education (NERCHE). (2014). *Definition of engaged scholarship.* Retrieved from http://www.nerche.org/index.php?option=com_content&view=article&id=265&catid=28

Nonaka, I., & Takeuchi, H. (1995). *The knowledge creating company.* New York, NY: Oxford University Press.

Organization for Economic Co-operation and Development (OECD). (2002). *Cities and regions in the new learning economy.* Paris, France: Author.

Osborne, M., Kearns, P., & Yang, J. (2013). Learning cities: Developing inclusive, prosperous and sustainable urban communities. *International Review of Education, 59,* 409–423.

Peters, S. J., & Eatman, T. K. (2014). Afterword: Speaking and working in critically hopeful terms. In D. D. Cooper (Ed.), *Learning in the plural: Essays on the humanities and public life* (pp. 167–178). East Lansing: Michigan State University Press.

Pinzon, D. P., & Arceo, F. D. B. (2006). Critical thinking in a higher education service-learning program. In K. M. Casey, G. Davidson, S. H. Billig, & N. C. Springer (Eds.), *Advancing knowledge in service learning: Research to transform the field* (pp. 89–110). Charlotte, NC: Information Age Publishing.

Stage, F. K., & Wells, R. S. (Eds.). (2014). *New Directions in Institutional Research: No. 158. New scholarship in critical quantitative research—Part 1: Studying institutions and people in context.* San Francisco, CA: Jossey-Bass.

Taleb, N. N. (2010). *The black swan: The impact of the highly improbable* (2nd ed.). New York, NY: Random House.

UNESCO Institute for Lifelong Learning. (2014, October). *Conference Report: International Conference on Learning Cities: Lifelong learning for all.* Hamburg, Germany: Author.

Wilkinson, R. G., & Pikett, K. (2009). *The spirit level: Why greater equality makes societies stronger.* London, UK: Allen Lane.

HIRAM E. FITZGERALD *is an associate provost for University Outreach and Engagement, and university distinguished professor in the Department of Psychology at Michigan State University.*

RENEE ZIENTEK *is the director of the Center for Service Learning and Civic Engagement at Michigan State University.*

3

Interconnections between workplace and organizational learning can highlight the ongoing changes taking place that prestage the need for learning cities and regions. The diverse institutions that comprise cities and regions can function as organizational learning mechanisms in the 21st century. Learning cities themselves can also be conceptualized as societal learning organizations.

Workplace, Organizational, and Societal: Three Domains of Learning for 21st-Century Cities

Lyle Yorks, Jody Barto

The concept of learning cities, regions, and communities holds considerable potential for meeting peoples' needs for lifelong learning that is both vocationally and socially interconnected. This is driven by the intensifying pace of technological innovation, subsequent globalization, changing demographics, escalating tensions between societies, and increasing complexity and uncertainty of life and learning. Realizing this potential will require drawing on the interconnections between adult education and human resource development, as citizens being learners are confronted with both the challenges of workplace change and the interconnectedness of communities.

Meeting these challenges will in part require drawing on the practices embedded in workplace and organizational learning, along with the challenges of making these practices workable. In doing so, it will be critical to address the often challenging need for balancing the creation of interinstitutional connections that serve people while enabling them to contribute to organizations and society in ways that have meaning for them. We turn now to discussing workplace and organizational learning, and the effects that emergent socioeconomic trends have for learning practices in these areas, with the intention of drawing out implications for the idea of learning cities.

Workplace and Organizational Learning

Workplace learning and organizational learning, respectively, are often associated with interrelated concepts such as lifelong learning, team learning,

New Directions for Adult and Continuing Education, no. 145, Spring 2015 © 2015 Wiley Periodicals, Inc.
Published online in Wiley Online Library (wileyonlinelibrary.com) • DOI: 10.1002/ace.20120

societal learning, and learning cities/regions. The word learning is common to all of these concepts irrespective of the framing and focus of interest raising the question "what is learning?" Many adult learning theorists have provided a number of frameworks that differentiate among types of learning along different dimensions (e.g., Argyris & Schön, 1978; Cell, 1984; Illeris, 2007, 2011; Jarvis, 2010; Marsick & Watkins, 1990; Mezirow, 1991; Yorks & Kasl, 2002).

Broadly defined concepts about learning range from very instrumental involving learning-specific skills and methods, to expanding one's range of knowledge and experiences within existing taken-for-granted frames of reference, to transformative changes in one's frame of reference through reflection on assumptions and reframing one's experiences. Additionally, learning is also conceptualized as developing a more complex way of making meaning, changing how the learner is in relationship to, and capable of making meaning of, the various social systems that comprise his or her lifeworld. All of these kinds of learning are relevant to workplace learning and, by extension, learning organizations, societal learning, and learning cities.

Workplace Learning. In the common vernacular of the past, up to perhaps the early to middle 20th century, "work" and "learning" were concepts regarding separate domains. "Work was about producing or doing things to earn a living. Learning was about education; it occurred in life before work. Training might be necessary at first in the workplace, but everything else that was needed for a lifetime employment could be picked up from experienced fellow workers" (Boud & Garrick, 1999, pp. 1–2). This observation brings into focus that learning in the workplace is not a new phenomenon; people were always learning in the workplace (Rowden, 1996). Rowden, citing Pace, Smith, and Mills (1991), notes that as early as possibly A.D. 1100, crafts, training, guilds, and apprenticeships were mechanisms for learning in working environments.

With the advent of the industrial revolution, training became increasingly formalized within organizations with an emphasis on efficiency. By the middle of the 20th century, gradual shifts in the workplace took place as markets began to become more international along with the emergence of more sophisticated manufacturing technologies. "Knowledge workers" became a phrase heard across industries, and lifelong learning became an important focus of attention both among higher education institutions and employers. While the trends differed across nations, settings and practices such as corporate universities, communities of practice, and organizations partnering with universities for customized management development and more specialized workshops became part of the territory of workplace learning.

As the competitive landscape has become one of the rapid changes driven by new technologies, and companies increasingly reorganize and/or change strategies, many have began to focus their learning-oriented activities on executive coaching as a primary method of executive development, changing the career trajectory of learning and development professionals (Passmore & Fillery-Travis, 2011). Along with these changes, more and more organizations expect potential hires to come with the competencies they project the organization needs to be competitive. Increasingly, there is a gap in accessing needed knowledge and skills "for non-privileged employees who receive little or no training, or must seek out their own education and training using their limited time and resources" (Watkins & Marsick, 2009, p. 132).

Adapting organizational workplace learning practices to the rapidly changing environment is complicated by the generational shifts taking place, shifts that have linked workplace learning and development with the broader need for talent management (Yorks & Abel, 2013). The millennial generation is entering employment in vast numbers and by 2020 they are expected to comprise 50% of the global workforce (Nicolaides, 2013). Millenials are generally well educated and, in comparison to Baby Boomers and Generation X, have additional skills with regard to the use of broadband, social media, and smartphones, along with an expectation for instant information on many issues (Myers & Sadaghiani, 2010; Nicolaides, 2013). This younger generation of adults is "increasingly coming into contact with social issues and needs, including the importance of the worker as opposed to the organization in which he or she is employed, the financial economic crisis plaguing the world and the values and social responsibility of their employer" (Nicolaides, 2013, p. 644). The constant change in the workplace learning terrain has implications for the need for organizational learning and increasingly societal learning.

Organizational Learning. During the latter half of the 20th century, workplace learning practices have broadened to emphasize employee and management development. Learning has come to be seen as not just something that takes place within individuals but as a relational process between people—giving rise to the question of whether groups or even organizations could learn. In the 1970s, the idea of organizational learning became a topic of debate within organizational theory. At the center of this debate was the issue of anthropomorphism—attributing human qualities to social structures (Popper & Lipshitz, 1998). March and Olsen (1976) argued that the concept of learning implies thought and the concept of organizational learning attributed human cognitive qualities to organizational structures.

Recognizing the dilemma of anthropomorphism, yet also understanding the reality that explaining why some organizations consistently adapt, innovate, or respond more effectively as a system, requires an organizational level of analysis beyond solely the individual; Popper, Lipshitz, and Friedman (Lipshitz, Friedman, & Popper, 2007; Lipshitz, Popper, & Friedman, 2002; Popper & Lipshitz, 1998) began developing a structural- and cultural-based model of organizational learning. Distinguishing between learning in organizations (LIO)—individuals learning from their experience and participation in learning-intended events—and learning by organizations (LBO)—various learning process that occur outside people's heads—Popper, Lipshitz, and Friedman proposed the concept of organization learning mechanisms (OLMs). Organization learning mechanisms are structured workplace learning processes that intentionally relate LIO to LBO through use of individual and team learning practices with the intention of having a productive impact on the organization through disseminating the learning. Examples of OLMs would be after action reviews, learning communities, coaching networks, and peer assists. OLMs can be formal or informal (self-organized) structures that combine individual learning that becomes collectively manifested within the group and is documented and disseminated, resulting in productive organizational change in strategy, tactics, policies, or operating procedures.

Enacting OLMs. Enacting OLMs requires the creation of spaces for adaptive and generative learning through the application of adult learning practices by establishing an organizational culture that enables the LIO to LBO connection. In the organization learning literature, adaptive learning is about coping with and adjusting existing practices, products, and services to changes in the environment; generative learning is about creating disruptive, innovative change (Chiva, Grandio, & Alegre, 2010; Christensen, Baumann, Ruggles, & Sadtler, 2006; Fiol & Lyles, 1985; Senge, 1990). Generative learning involves questioning the assumptions that inform how we frame situations and guides our actions (Mezirow, 1991) through processes of relating new knowledge and experiences to prior ones leading to new insights and transformed practices (Nevis, DiBella, & Gould, 1995; Wittrock, 1974).

Adult learning practices necessary for such learning require establishing a culture of open dialogue among people and groups that hold different frames of references and have different perceived interests. Lipshitz et al. (2007) describe key elements of such a culture: (a) *Inquiry*—persisting in investigation and suspending "judgment until full understanding is achieved" (p. 48); (b) *Issue orientation*—"focusing the learning on a specific issue or problem" (p. 51) and considering "the relevance of information irrespective of the social standing or rank of the person giving or receiving this information" (p. 53); (c) *Transparency*—exposing "one's actions and thoughts to the scrutiny of others" (p. 53); (d) *Integrity*—"admitting errors in judgment or action when shown compelling evidence to that effect, even at the risk of incurring some costs as a consequence" (pp. 56–58); and (e) *Accountability*—taking "responsibility for learning and for the implementation of lessons learned" (p. 60).

Establishing such a culture is challenging. It requires leadership that models a tolerance for error, treating errors as learning opportunities, deemphasizing status differences, and promoting personal safety. The latter is particularly challenging in a climate of rapid organizational change where job security is a fleeting dream.

Further understanding of the complexity of creating OLMs is made clear through the empirically based team learning model developed by Kasl, Marsick, and Dechant (1997). Kasl et al. (1997) describe four learning modes that take place within teams: (a) *fragmented*—individual learning is not shared with or by others; (b) *pooled*—individuals share information and perspectives and small subgroupings within the team learn together, but the team as a whole does not learn; (c) *synergistic learning*—the group as a whole creates knowledge mutually, integrating divergent perspectives in new ways with team knowledge being integrated into individual meaning schemes; and (d) *continuous learning*—where "synergistic learning becomes habitual" (p. 231). To have effective organizational learning taking place, mode (c) needs to be a regular occurrence; ideally mode (d) becomes an element of the culture. Kasl et al. (1997) identify three learning conditions that map onto the more specific cultural norms posited by Lipshitz et al. (2007): (a) appreciation of team work—openness to hearing the ideas of others and the extent to which members value playing a team role; (b) individual expression, including having the opportunity to give input in forming goals and being able to express objections; and (c) operating principles—having established commonly held values, norms, and structure.

Organizational learning requires crossing boundaries across the larger organization and many times between OLMs. This means that the team learning conditions described above have to become part of the organization's culture. There needs to be leadership support for the operation of teams and other OLMs with collaboration across the organization (Dechant, Marsick, & Kasl, 1993). Both the need for and the challenge of enacting organizational learning are becoming more complex with increasing globalization. National and regional cultures have a strong influence on the manifestation of OLMs (Yorks, 2003).

While we have focused on business organizations, organizational learning can take place in all sectors of society. For example, Gephart and Marsick (in press) have researched how leadership at a high school transformed the school, eliminating tracking of students by performance and teaching all students rigorous, honors curricula. The result was improved achievement for all students and a closing of the historic White–non-White achievement gap. Longworth (2006) describes how organizational learning structures and principles, applied to municipal agencies and schools, are integral to creating learning cities and regions.

OLMs as Learning Systems. Workplace learning and organizational learning are interconnected—two dimensions of a systemic process involving individuals, groups (both informal and formal), and the organization. Many workplace learning initiatives are focused on individuals; others on teams or groups. Organizational learning requires that many workplace learning initiatives become OLMs that integrate LIO and LBO. This integration requires establishing a culture that is supportive of synergistic team learning conditions. These dimensions of the learning system have always been periodically informally or incidentally interacting.

The transition from an industrial-based economy to a digital-technology-based economy has confronted organizations with a new set of challenges adding to the complexity that individuals and organizations have to learn their way through in the context of increasing rapid change. As citizens and economies are confronted by these challenges, an increasing need for societal learning comes to the forefront to establish OLM's crossing organizational and institutional boundaries.

New Directions for Adult and Continuing Education • DOI: 10.1002/ace

The Role of Societal Learning

Fox and Brown (1998) define societal learning as "articulating new paradigms that can alter the perspectives, goals, and behaviors of social systems larger than particular organizations" (p. 474) such as cities. Cities, like organizations, are comprised of formal and informal systems of relationships confronted with the need for societal learning through continual change. Like individual, team, and organizational learning, societal learning "involves cycles of observe-reflect-plan-act and produces new capacity for learning. However, it works at a much larger scale because the new capacity is societal" and in doing so requires developing "new relationships, strategies, and organizational structure to do what could not be done before" (Waddell, 2002, p. 18).

Organizational, institutional, community, and societal structures shape the possibilities for learning through constraining or opening up social connections. Society and organizations place substantial barriers in the way of processes for learning (Fisher & Torbert, 1995). Societal learning requires penetrating these barriers by creating a learning culture, or subculture, of inquiry that mirrors Lipshitz et al.'s (2007) five elements of *Inquiry*, *Issue-orientation*, *Transparency*, *Integrity*, and *Accountability*. OLMs need to function as what Fisher and Torbert (1995) refer to as *liberating structures* that are "both productive and educate members toward self-correcting awareness" (p. 7) through engaging in collaborative action inquiry for the generation of new meaning (Yorks, 2005).

While organizational learning can be challenging, establishing such a societal culture can be more so. However, organizations and institutions are facing intensifying new, contemporary demands from various sectors of society that can be leveraged to move them toward such a culture. The advent of the digital age is confronting organizations with learning challenges beyond workplace learning and talent management, specifically more transparency, and a growing public demand for organizations to be more socially responsible. The dramatic expansion of the Internet, since the U.S. Congress passed the High Performance Computing and Communication Act in 1991, has allowed for the ways in which corporations operate to become increasingly transparent to the public (Coombs & Holladay, 2013). The Internet provides a platform for corporate actions to be open to stakeholder inspection even when they might attempt to conceal them (Goleman, 2009). It also ensures that irresponsible actions on behalf of corporations will be exposed and punished (Coombs & Holladay, 2013). The Public Affairs Council posits that the Internet has enabled "activists groups to show video of human rights abuses and create databases that help citizens figure out which companies are polluting the air in their neighborhood" (Pinkham, 2010, para. 12).

These pressures are themselves part of a gradual process of societal learning intensified by the generational shift that is taking place in the workforce. How organizations respond to these changing societal expectations is in turn what drives their potential successes or failures (Zadek, 2006). The ways in which organizations respond to these expectations "can impact on how business as a whole functions within the system, which in turn evolves as a result" (p. 339). Zadek posits five learning stages a company moves through: defensive, compliance, managerial, strategic, and civil learning. In the civil learning stage, "companies find themselves actively engaged in lobbying for public policies that are supportive of their increasingly 'responsible' practices" (p. 340). We also note that it is important to acknowledge the extent of the challenge in getting corporations to begin learning their way through these stages. Doing so depends on how individuals learn and take action through diverse institutions, leveraging the insights provided by digital technology.

Expanding the Learning System: Learning Cities, Regions, and States

As societal learning has driven the increasing demand for organizations to be socially responsible, new needs for organizational learning are apparent. While profitability of private sector organizations and satisfying the core constituencies of nonprofits such as social service organizations, advocacy groups, religious and educational institutions, among others, remain the center of their attention, meeting these new challenges requires interacting with the broader community in a fundamentally different way, going beyond lobbying legislators and public relations campaigns.

Learning cities can themselves be conceptualized as learning organizations (Longworth, 2006). While one way of defining learning cities involves applying learning organization practices to civic and/or educational institutions to train and educate their staff in the need and ways to provide their citizens with lifelong learning opportunities, there is a more holistic sense in which cities and regions themselves, through a collective of administration departments, businesses, suppliers, and citizens, "form a vibrant and symbiotic learning organization" (Longworth, 2006, p. 30). Doing so requires what are, in effect, OLMs—spaces that facilitate a learning connection between individuals and the organizations or social entities which they are a part of, with the long-term result being societal learning.

Such OLMs could be in the form of collaborative cross-organization task forces that in turn interface with, or are comprised of members from, other OLMs in their respective settings. Members of such task forces must evolve from a focus on protecting their organizational or institutional interests to balancing or integrating and reframing these interests with those of other organizations and institutions in the interest. Moving from fragmented, to pooled, and then synergistic learning (Kasl et al., 1997) involves establishing an evolving relationship among members of the OLMs through repetitive cycles of action and reflection through engaging in inquiry.

This, we admit, is a very ambitious vision given the bifurcated nature of significant segments of contemporary societies. But some examples of movement in this direction are taking place. Byun & Ryu (2012) describe South Korea's Life Long Cities Project "based on the Life Long Education Law promulgated in 1999," the purpose of which "is to provide everyone with suitable learning opportunities at anytime and anywhere, to improve the quality of life, and to contribute to social development" (pp. 281–282). One example is Gwangmyeong Lifelong Learning Center, which partners with the Social Solidarity Bank, the Social Welfare Center, and the division for social welfare with the municipal government of the city. The center took charge of the overall process of program development and program operation; the bank took charge of training for start-ups and business management and helped start businesses; and the Welfare Center, the division for social welfare, took care of participants who wished to start their own business by consulting with them. "As a result of the program, some participants who had been homeless are now running their own businesses such as cleaning service companies and groceries. The program showed the possibility of a synergy effect that can be created through partnership among education, labor, and welfare" (p. 283).

In another example, South Carolina's on-the-job training program offers a $1,000 annual tax credit for each apprentice on the payroll. Increasingly, apprenticeships are reemerging as a form of workplace learning, providing quality learning through real jobs. Projecting worker shortages in health care and advanced manufacturing, the state has made the tax credit as user friendly as possible (Weber, 2014).

For learning cities and regions to be developed through these kinds of partnerships across sectors, the participating organizations need to engage in conversational spaces that function as cross-organizational OLMs bringing together the learning taking place within each organization and institution with shared synergistic learning across the partnership system in the service of the broader societal–cultural perspective. Key learning needs to be captured and disseminated in the larger social space with the intention of creating a more inquiry-based culture. Cities and states need to become learning spaces as well as political ones.

Workplace and organizational learning practices can be applied at interorganizational and societal levels of the learning system. Doing so, however, means applying them in a meaningful way within organizations and institutions. Higher education institutions need to incorporate collaborative action inquiry into their curriculums through experiential learning pedagogies (Yorks & Nicolaides, 2013). Ultimately, creating and participating in OLMs for organizational and societal learning require people having the intentions and skills for enacting a learning culture. Fostering learning cities requires that learning is taking place at all levels, individual, team, organizational, and societal. One of the authors continues to remember a comment made by adult educator Jack Mezirow during a class discussion with graduate students more than 20 years ago: "People shouldn't be resources for organizations; organizations should be resources for people." To rephrase Mezirow's comment, cities and regions, and the organizations and institutions that comprise them, need to be resources for their citizens, allowing their citizens to contribute back to these organizations and institutions.

References

Argyris, C., & Schön, D. A. (1978). *Organizational learning: A theory of action perspective.* Reading, MA: Addison-Wesley.

Boud, D., & Garrick J. (1999). Understandings of workplace learning. In D. Boud & J. Garrick (Ed.), *Understanding learning at work* (pp. 1–11). New York, NY: Routledge.

Byun, J., & Ryu, K. (2012). Changes in regional communities: The case of the Republic of Korea's Lifelong Learning City Project. *Advances in Developing Human Resources, 14*(3), 279–290.

Cell, E. (1984). *Learning to learn from experience.* Albany: State University of New York Press.

Chiva, R., Grandio, A., & Alegre, J. (2010). Adaptive and generative learning: Implications from complexity theories. *International Journal of Management Reviews, 12*(2), 114–129.

Christensen, C. M., Baumann, H., Ruggles, R., & Sadtler, T. M. (2006). Disruptive innovation for social change. *Harvard Business Review, 75*(6), 94–101.

Coombs, W. T., & Holladay, S. J. (2013). *It's not just PR: Public relations in society.* Hoboken, NJ: Wiley.

Dechant, K., Marsick, V. J., & Kasl, E. (1993). Towards a model of team learning. *Studies in Continuing Education, 15*(1), 1–14.

Fiol, M. C., & Lyles, M. A. (1985). Organizational learning. *Academy of Management Review, 10,* 803–813.

Fisher, D., & Torbert, W. R. (1995). *Personal and organizational transformations: The true challenge of continual quality improvement.* London, UK: McGraw-Hill.

Fox, J., & Brown, L. D. (1998). *The struggle for accountability: The World Bank, NGOs, and grassroots movements.* Cambridge, MA: MIT Press.

Gephart, M., & Marsick, V. J. (in press). *Strategic organizational learning.* Berlin, Germany: Springer.

Goleman, D. (2009). *Winning in an age of radical transparency.* Retrieved from http://blogs.hbr.org/leadinggreen/2009/05/radical-transparency.html

Illeris, K. (2007). *How we learn: Learning and non-learning in school and beyond.* London, UK: Routledge.

Illeris, K. (2011). *The fundamentals of workplace learning: Understanding how people learn in working life.* London, UK: Routledge.

Jarvis, P. (2010). *Adult education and lifelong learning: Theory and practice* (4th ed.). New York, NY: Routledge.

Kasl, E., Marsick, V. J., & Dechant, K. (1997). Teams as learners: A research-based model of team learning. *The Journal of Applied Behavioral Science, 33*(2), 227–246.

Lipshitz, R., Friedman, V. J., & Popper, M. (2007). *Demystifying organizational learning.* Thousand Oaks, CA: Sage.

Lipshitz, R., Popper, M., & Friedman, V. (2002). A multi-facet model of organizational learning. *Journal of Applied Behavioral Science, 38,* 78–98.

Longworth, N. (2006). *Learning cities, learning regions, learning communities: Lifelong learning and local government.* London, UK: Routledge.

March, J. G., & Olsen, J. P. (1976). *Ambiguity and choice in organizations.* Bergen, Norway: Universitetsforlaget.

Marsick, V. J., & Watkins, K. E. (1990). *Informal and incidental learning in the workplace.* London, UK: Routledge.

Mezirow, J. (1991). *Transformative dimensions of adult learning.* San Francisco, CA: Jossey-Bass.

Myers, K. K., & Sadaghiani, K. (2010). Millenials in the workplace: A communication perspective on millenials' organizational relationships and performance. *Business and Psychology, 25*(2), 225–238.

Nevis, E. C., DiBella, A. J., & Gould, J. M. (1995). Understanding organizations as learning systems. *Sloan Management Review, 36*(2), 73–85.

Nicolaides, A. (2013). Quo vadis corporate social responsibility in an age dominated by millenials. *Educational Research, 4*(9), 642–653.

Pace, R. W., Smith, P. C., & Mills, G. E. (1991). *Human resource development: The field.* Englewood Cliffs, NJ: Prentice-Hall.

Passmore, J., & Fillery-Travis, A. (2011). A critical review of executive coaching research: A decade of progress and what's to come. *Coaching: An International Journal of Theory, Research and Practice, 4*(2), 70–88.

Pinkham, D. (2010). *A guide to corporate transparency.* Retrieved from http://pac.org /ethics/a-guide-to-corporate-transparency

Popper, M., & Lipshitz, R. (1998). Organizational learning mechanisms a structural and cultural approach to organizational learning. *The Journal of Applied Behavioral Science, 34*(2), 161–178.

Rowden, R. (1996). Current realities and future challenges. In R. W. Rowden (Ed.), *Workplace learning: Debating five critical questions of theory and practice* (pp. 3–10). San Francisco, CA: Jossey-Bass.

Senge, P. M. (1990). *The fifth discipline: The art and practice of the learning organization.* New York, NY: Doubleday/Currency.

Waddell, S. J. (2002). Six societal learning concepts for a new era of engagement. *Reflections, 3*(4), 18–27.

Watkins, K. E., & Marsick, V. J. (2009). Trends in lifelong learning in the US workplace. In P. Jarvis (Ed.), *The Routledge international handbook of lifelong learning* (pp. 129–138). Abingdon, Oxford, UK: Routledge.

Weber, L. (2014, April 28). Here's one way to solve the skills gap: Apprenticeships can help give companies the employees they need. So why aren't there more of them? *The Wall Street Journal,* R3.

Wittrock, M. C. (1974). Learning as a generative process. *Educational Psychologist, 11*, 87–95.

Yorks, L. (Ed.). (2003). *Cross-cultural dimensions of team learning. Advances in developing human resources series* (Vol. 5[1]). Thousand Oaks, CA: Sage.

Yorks, L. (2005). Adult learning and the generation of new knowledge and meaning: Creating liberating spaces for fostering adult learning through practitioner-based collaborative action inquiry. *Teachers College Record, 107*(6), 1217–1244.

Yorks, L., & Abel, A. (2013). *Strategic talent management: Where we need to go.* New York, NY: The Conference Board.

Yorks, L., & Kasl, E. (2002). Toward a theory and practice for whole-person learning: Reconceptualizing experience and the role of affect. *Adult Education Quarterly, 52*, 176–192.

Yorks, L., & Nicolaides, A. (2013). Toward an integral approach for evolving mindsets for generative learning and timely action in the midst of ambiguity. *Teachers College Record, 115*(8), 1–26.

Zadek, S. (2006). Responsible competitiveness: Reshaping global markets through responsible business practices. *Corporate Governance, 6*(4), 334–348.

LYLE YORKS *is an associate professor in the Department of Organization and Leadership, Teachers College, Columbia University.*

JODY BARTO *is the founder and principal consultant for Jody Barto, Adult Learning Strategist and Coach, LLC. She is also adjunct faculty at Fairleigh Dickinson University and Manhattan College.*

4

This chapter examines the parallel histories and visions of public libraries and land-grant universities' Cooperative Extension in providing lifelong learning opportunities; it illustrates how partnerships between organizations can enhance the vibrancy of adult education in the context of learning cities.

Public Libraries and Cooperative Extension as Community Partners for Lifelong Learning and Learning Cities

Alysia Peich, Cynthia Needles Fletcher

Public libraries and Cooperative Extension, the outreach arm of land-grant universities, provide nonformal adult education opportunities in communities large and small across the United States. Both institutions are vital to the development and advancement of learning cities, where organizations unite to meet the needs of individuals and the community and create a more educated citizenry. An examination of the histories of these two institutions reveals similarities between the visions of both to provide education to underserved communities. By expanding lifelong learning opportunities, public libraries and Cooperative Extension have strived to serve the learning needs of society. While providing educational opportunities to individuals, public libraries and Cooperative Extension can also serve the greater educational needs of communities. Working together, these organizations have even greater reach, particularly in rural communities in which public libraries and Extension may provide some of the only nonformal educational opportunities for adults. In Iowa, a recent partnership between Iowa Library Services (IaLS), which is the state library, and Iowa State University Extension and Outreach (ISUEO) brought financial education to 43 rural communities across the state between 2010 and 2013.

This chapter examines the parallel visions of public libraries and Cooperative Extension, historically and in the present, to provide lifelong learning opportunities to communities. The Smart investing@your library® project (Peich & Fletcher, 2013), a collaboration between IaLS and ISUEO, provides an example of how cooperation between organizations contributed to learning

NEW DIRECTIONS FOR ADULT AND CONTINUING EDUCATION, no. 145, Spring 2015 © 2015 Wiley Periodicals, Inc.
Published online in Wiley Online Library (wileyonlinelibrary.com) • DOI: 10.1002/ace.20122

cities across Iowa by providing unbiased, high-quality financial education to rural communities (FINRA Investor Education Foundation, 2014).

Vision of Public Libraries and Land-Grant Universities in the 19th Century

A vision of public libraries as providers of lifelong learning opportunities can be found as early as the late 19th century. Adams (1887) suggested that every public library should be "a people's university, the highest of high schools in the community," and encouraged public librarians to take an active role in providing adult education (p. 25). At a time when higher education was unattainable for many, Adams envisioned a public institution where all people, irrespective of social position, could extend their learning into adulthood. In addition to making this early connection between lifelong adult learning and libraries, Adams (1887) also suggested a relationship between libraries and what he refers to as "university extension" (p. 21). Describing extension of English universities at the time, Adams broadly referred to university extension as providing an "extension of higher education by the classes to the masses" (p. 29).

Adams (1887) recommended the adoption of a similar model in the United States, but associated with public libraries rather than universities. Adams believed that extending education to the masses could "be accomplished in America through the agency of our great public libraries, by utilizing the highest educational forces within their reach" (p. 26). For Adams, public libraries could extend similar educational opportunities offered by institutions of higher education to people for whom higher education was out of reach.

The history and evolution of land-grant universities and their outreach to lifelong learners have many parallels with the history of public libraries' role in lifelong learning. In the early 19th century, colleges and universities educated the elites of U.S. society and were strongly influenced by European models focused on classical and professional education. By the mid-19th century, higher education remained widely unavailable to many agricultural and industrial workers (Brunner, 1962; NASULGC, 1995). In 1862, President Lincoln signed the Morrill Act, which provided grants for land to states to establish "at least one college ... to promote the liberal and practical education of the industrial classes in the several pursuits and profession in life" (First Morrill Act, 1862). These land-grant universities were established as people's universities based on the principle "that no part of human life and labor is beneath the notice of the university or without its proper dignity" (McDowell, 2001, p. 3).

Soon there was recognition that teaching and education needed to be augmented with ongoing research capabilities. The Hatch Act of 1887 funded research farms where the universities could conduct applied studies, primarily related to agriculture, mechanics, and rural life. Since their inception, the hallmark of land-grant universities has been research-based education that responds to economic and social change. Today, there is at least one land-grant institution in every state and major territory of the United States that "extends" the university's educational resources to urban as well as rural communities to address contemporary lifelong learning needs through Cooperative Extension Service programs.

Public Libraries as Centers for Adult Education in the 20th Century

Some chronologies mark the 1920s as the earliest milestone in the history of public libraries moving forward with Adams's vision of libraries as people's universities to actively provide lifelong and adult learning opportunities (Gilton, 2012; Lee, 1966; Monroe, 1963; Monroe & Heim, 1991; Norman, 2012). However, as early as the beginning of the 20th century, librarians began to consider the public library as a more integral part of the education system (Lee, 1966, p. 40). For example, public libraries began to play a prominent role in the development of literacy skills, which was vital to ensure that the growing numbers of new Americans, without access to formal education, developed literacy skills to succeed in their new country (Lee, 1966, p. 41). Librarians began to take a more active role in educating communities, advancing libraries beyond serving merely as storehouses of books.

The early years of the 20th century also saw a boom in public library construction across the country. This has been attributed in large part to the efforts of the Carnegie Foundation (Bobinski, 1969). Carnegie viewed public libraries as "major agencies for adult education in the United States" (Monroe, 1963, p. 27). In a review of the progress of Carnegie's efforts, Johnson (1938) called attention to the responsibility of public libraries to provide what he referred to as a "people's university" (p. 71). In his report on the influence of Carnegie's efforts, Johnson described the public library as having risen "upon a foundation of adult education. Its great expansion came with the extension of the adult educational impulse to the masses" (p. 27). Johnson was not a librarian, but he identified adult education as one of the most important roles of public libraries, which was communicated throughout the Carnegie Foundation. Johnson also suggested that the future of libraries would be adult education. He reported to Carnegie that public libraries' "prestige in the present and its hopes for the future rest upon the explicitness and effectiveness of its adult educational activities" (Johnson, 1938, p. 27).

In the 1920s, as interest in adult education grew in both public libraries and land-grant universities, Learned (1924) made a connection between the goals of university extension and public libraries. Learned and others' use of the term "university extension" was nonspecific, simply referring to an extension of education outside university walls, and did not refer specifically to Cooperative Extension programs being developed at land-grant universities. In support of university extension courses, the type of library envisioned by Learned (1924) "would provide a home and tools, together with whatever cooperation of staff members might be desirable" (p. 21). Further developing this image of the public library as provider of adult education, Learned (1924) emphasized that because it is "less formal, less governed by tradition, and wholly uninterested in any examinations, credit or degrees," the public library "would constitute the first powerful and aggressive community agency for education" (p. 22). Public libraries became institutions positioned to extend learning opportunities outside of universities to people without access to formal education.

Enthusiasm for public libraries as centers for adult education was shared by librarians in the years between WWI and WWII. According to Lee (1966), increasing numbers of librarians during this time "were confirmed in the belief that they were capable of employing their resources and their energies in direct educational processes" (p. 45). Librarians' enthusiasm about this role of public libraries aligned their mission of providing learning opportunities with federal initiatives designed to revitalize the national consciousness and the economy following WWII. The American Library Association (ALA, 1943) prepared *Post-War Standards for Public Libraries* in response to a request by the federal National Resources Planning Board (NRPB), which was created in 1939 as an outgrowth of New Deal domestic programs intended to stimulate public works through local, state, and regional planning (Clawson, 2013). By requesting the report from the ALA, the NRPB recognized public libraries as important institutions capable of contributing to rebuilding the United States following years of economic uncertainty and war.

The informal education provided by libraries was recognized as having the potential to develop a stronger citizenry by teaching literacy, job skills, and developing cultural knowledge. The *Post-War Standards for Public Libraries* (ALA, 1943) were explicit in their recognition of libraries as providers of adult education, and that "continuing education is essential in a democratic society" (p. 28). By establishing libraries as essential to democracy, the ALA made clear to the NRPB that libraries could contribute greatly to important postwar social and economic rebuilding, and do so largely through adult education and lifelong learning. The document does not simply recommend that public libraries provide the materials to support adult education; the first standard under adult education is that "Each library should develop an *active* [emphasis added] program for informal education" (p. 28). Public libraries have historically provided both informal and nonformal education (Gilton, 2012). Informal education, which lacks the structure and intentionality of the formal education provided by institutions such as public schools and universities, appears in libraries as access to resources and materials that support self-directed learning. Nonformal education, which mirrors the structure of education institutions but is facilitated outside of the traditional boundaries of formal education, is often facilitated by libraries and provided by partnering organizations. When Adams (1887) recommended that public libraries serve as an extension of universities, he envisioned libraries as providers of facilitators of nonformal education.

New Directions for Adult and Continuing Education • DOI: 10.1002/ace

Following WWII, Ditzion (1947) again recognized a connection between university extension and public libraries. Ditzion wrote that university extension "held a position of great esteem among librarians; its own partisans recognized the high value of free public libraries in the adult education process" (p. 81). In his work on the role of public libraries in the United States, Leigh (1950) describes a different relationship between university extension and public libraries than the Adams vision. Leigh (1950) reported "as yet the public library has not been widely used as the official materials and program center for more formally-organized adult education groups under the auspices of public schools, universities and agricultural extension agencies" (p. 233). However, Leigh (1950) recognized that public libraries could serve formal education organizations by providing resources and space (p. 233). By suggesting that public libraries operate in conjunction with more formal educational organizations, Leigh recommended collaboration. What Leigh referred to as agricultural extension is today called Cooperative Extension. Partnerships between public libraries and Cooperative Extension, such as the one between Iowa public libraries and ISUEO, fulfill Leigh's vision of the potential role of libraries in lifelong education.

Just as public libraries began taking a more active role in lifelong learning in the early 1900s, land-grant universities assumed more responsibility for providing nonformal education. In 1914, the Smith–Lever Act provided federal support through the Department of Agriculture for land-grant universities to offer nonformal, noncredit educational programs beyond their campuses through Cooperative Extension programs that were developed and funded jointly by states and local communities. The term "Cooperative Extension System" describes the partnership of federal, state, and local communities to support research-based lifelong learning emanating from the land-grant universities. When established 100 years ago, Extension addressed exclusively rural and agricultural issues. Soon after its formal inception in 1914, Cooperative Extension gained visibility and stature in rural areas by working with farmers and rural families to increase production and conservation of food during WWI. Local Extension educators became known for working directly with learners and for using multiple teaching methods in nonformal settings. By 1920, home economics Extension educators "used various means of presenting material including traditional lectures, demonstration lectures, exhibits, fairs, films and slides, style shows, plays, conferences, printed material, and work with boys' and girls' clubs" to address areas of clothing, food, home furnishings, home management, and health (Knowles, 1920, p. 2). Once again, during WWII, Extension responded to the need to help increase production and preservation of food as well as other needs brought on by the onset of war. Bliss (1960), a long-time administrator, observed Extension "adapting its educational programs to changing conditions and to emergencies" (p. 205).

The latter half of the 20th century was a period in which Cooperative Extension expanded its focus to meet the needs of urban as well as rural communities. Community resource development and public affairs education, grounded in the universities' applied research, addressed identified local needs. At the 75th anniversary of the inception of Iowa State University Extension, Schweider (1993) chronicled the organization's rich history, marked by a "continual process of change" to meet societal needs, and pondered its future. Anderson (as cited in Schweider, 1993) observed a shift in the 1950s and 1960s to a more formalized educational system and described extension educators as the "architects of information *education* [emphasis added]" who dealt not just with transmission of facts but with an educational process (p. 218). Powers (as cited in Schweider, 1993) concurred with this important differentiation and mused about the future of Cooperative Extension: "There will come a time when people will say, 'You know, we've got hundreds of sources of information but nobody who can explain this [material] or help me sort out or make choices and that's what we want ... Extension to do, because that's what your job is'" (p. 228). Powers's prescience has been born out today as Extension educators help adult learners make meaning out of information, use it to make informed decisions, and develop knowledge and skills. However, it is through community partnerships that Extension is better able to achieve its goals and contribute to 21st-century learning cities. Such university–community partnerships expand outreach to diverse and underserved audiences, leverage the resources of the partners, and enhance the vibrancy of adult lifelong learning.

Public Libraries and Cooperative Extension as 21st-Century Community Partners

Today, mission statements of public libraries frequently refer to lifelong learning. One of the defining characteristics of public libraries is that they are open to all people, irrespective of background or age. The access to space and resources that public libraries provide supports a variety of lifelong learning opportunities for adults, from entirely self-directed to semistructured. In public libraries, adults have access to resources that, depending on interest or need, are specific and available "on demand" for informal, self-directed learning. In addition to the physical items that are available during operating hours, public libraries have access to online resources that are available at any time. Public library programming provides more structured, nonformal learning opportunities that may include computer instruction, lectures about cultural topics, or classes such as Smart investing@your library®. Because of the space, programs, and access to resources that they provide, "Adult learners are the norm in public libraries" and as a result services to them should not be overlooked or undervalued (Gilton, 2012, p. 191). Contemporary public libraries have proven valuable at providing lifelong learning in response to rapidly changing developments in technology, volatile economies, and shifting demographics. Many of these changes result in a need for communities to learn what are considered 21st-century skills. In 2009, the Institute of Museum and Library Services (IMLS) published *Museums, Libraries and 21st Century Skills*, which both defined the necessary skills and provided examples of how libraries and

New Directions for Adult and Continuing Education • DOI: 10.1002/ace

museums ensure individuals are prepared with the skills necessary to thrive in a new century. Twenty-first-century skills range from information and financial literacy, to interpersonal and technology skills, to civic education. In addition to including skills that serve individual needs, such as securing employment and using technology, 21st-century skills include those that serve the needs of communities. Civic education and engagement, for example, serve individuals by preparing them to not only participate in civic life, but also strengthen the success of democracy by producing well-informed voters. Financial literacy and employment preparedness serve both individual and societal economic needs. By providing the resources, programs, and partnerships that support 21st-century skills, public libraries meet the lifelong learning needs of both individuals and communities.

At the turn of the 21st century, McDowell (2001) assessed the future of land-grant universities and Cooperative Extension and claimed that the basic quest is to achieve a society "in which all have opportunity to learn broadly throughout a lifetime." Over time, land-grant universities have reaffirmed their commitment to this goal and resolved to reemphasize the importance of local partnerships. This emphasis on partnerships to achieve the goal of extending learning opportunities to all members of society is similar to the IMLS vision of the role of libraries in the 21st century. The IMLS (2009) cites lifelong learning as vital to its mission statement, and has placed "the learner at the center" as the first goal in its 2012–2016 strategic plan (IMLS, 2012, p. 5). In its recommendations to how libraries can place learners at the center, the IMLS suggests partnerships with community organizations.

Partnership of Iowa State University Extension and Outreach and Iowa Library Services. In Iowa, ISUEO and IaLS continued the historical connection between university extension and public libraries by partnering to develop the 21st-century skills of financial literacy in rural communities across the state. Smart investing@your library®, an initiative of the ALA and the Financial Industry Regulatory Authority (FINRA) Investor Education Foundation, provided funding for a statewide professional development and financial educational outreach project in public libraries in 43 communities. At a time when the financial recession left even the smallest communities uncertain about their economies, the Smart investing@your library® program provided Iowans with unbiased, high-quality financial education to strengthen their economic futures. Although the cities participating in the program were very rural with populations less than 25,000, the partnership between ISUEO and IaLS ensured rural residents of Iowa had access to the same quality of financial education as their fellow Americans living in large urban centers.

The Iowa Smart investing@your library® case study illustrates how public libraries, working with ISUEO partners, can build capacity to connect adult lifelong learners with appropriate information and timely learning opportunities (Peich & Fletcher, 2013). The goal of Smart investing@your library® was to provide personal finance and investing knowledge, skills, and tools to lifelong learners in underserved communities in rural Iowa. Financial literacy is identified as a 21st-century skill by IMLS (2009) and is important to both individual and community growth. Connecting individual growth with societal success, the mission of the FINRA Investor Education Foundation is to "provide underserved Americans with the knowledge, skills and tools necessary for financial success throughout life," and ultimately contribute to "a society characterized by universal financial literacy" (FINRA Investor Education Foundation, 2014). To meet the goal of contributing to individual and community financial health, Iowa's program included a six-week hybrid investing class, consisting of four online modules marked at the beginning and end by face-to-face meetings in the libraries. Although the development of the content and delivery of the project's course offerings fell primarily to the ISUEO faculty, the libraries were heavily involved in promotion of the program and ongoing support during the six-week period during which the classes were offered. The success of the program was evident in the course evaluation, which identified significant, positive outcomes for participants in knowledge gain, increased confidence in decision making, and improved skills in discussing investing with family members. The positive changes in individual knowledge gain and behavior illustrate the potential impact of the project on the financial knowledge of the participating communities.

In order to accomplish the goal of providing education toward financial literacy, the project developed professional development opportunities for librarians to support financial education outreach, expanded the personal finance collections of the libraries, and created targeted learning activities for library patrons. Each of these components contributed to the positive outcomes for both the librarians and participating community members. Libraries were identified as having the outreach, capacity, and resources to promote financial literacy, and ISUEO provided the subject matter and teaching expertise to deliver the classes. The partnership is reminiscent of what Leigh (1950) suggested when he described libraries as providing the resources and space for formal education "enterprises" (p. 233). The informality of the library as a learning environment, with librarians as course guides, provided an ideal place for delivering financial education.

Professional development for librarians was identified as important because the librarians served as informal guides between the structured classes in the program, they promoted the classes in their communities, and they were encouraged to develop additional partnerships with community organizations in order to sustain the financial literacy goals of the project. The librarians' professional development emphasized reference strategies in the use of appropriate personal finance and investing information tools and social marketing skills to connect lifelong learners with the library. Case study interviews with library workers in Wisconsin have identified librarians' own lack of financial knowledge, particularly awareness of information sources, as a problem that made reference interactions challenging. Despite their own perceived shortcomings in this subject area, the majority felt libraries have an important role to play in helping people in need of financial information (Arnot & Eschenfelder,

2011). Effective marketing skills are an ongoing challenge as libraries attempt to broaden their community outreach. Developing partnerships with other organizations is vital for libraries to leverage diminishing resources, particularly in small, financially challenged communities. IaLS and ISUEO worked together to design, implement, and evaluate professional development opportunities that prepared the participating librarians to carry out the program in their communities. The strengths of each partner contributed to a higher quality professional development experience than either entity could have developed on their own. By providing professional development, ISUEO and IaLS also looked toward the sustainability of developing librarians as facilitators of nonformal education. The participating librarians are now prepared with the skills to take a more active role in securing the library as a vital part of a learning city.

Based on the experience with the Iowa Smart investing@your library® project as well as quantitative and qualitative evaluation of each component of the project, ISUEO and IaLS drew several conclusions about how such partnerships might advance the concept of learning cities.

1. A commitment to ongoing professional development ensures that adult library patrons will continue to be guided by librarians toward high-quality references, will receive appropriate referrals to other community resources when needed, will access useful collections to inform lifelong learning needs, and will see the public library as a center for lifelong learning.
2. Organizations such as ISUEO will continue to consider public libraries as organizations vital to providing the space, expertise, and community access necessary to successfully carry out lifelong educational programming.
3. Effective and resourceful partnerships such as the one between Iowa public libraries and ISUEO can be critical to achieving libraries' and Cooperative Extension's long-term role in learning cities; however, communities will vary widely in potential partners.
4. Rural and other underserved communities will continue to be challenged to access the resources that can meet the diverse needs of adult library patrons.
5. Designing effective models for adult educational programming and outreach requires strong evaluation imbedded in program design.
6. Both formative and summative evaluations will guide libraries and the communities they serve in identifying needs and then designing and revising outreach strategies in a constantly changing environment.

Conclusion

Public libraries are integral members of learning cities because they strengthen the pervasive network of resources that provide lifelong learning. The Iowa

New Directions for Adult and Continuing Education • DOI: 10.1002/ace

public libraries that participated in Smart investing@your library®, like public libraries everywhere, continue to meet the diverse needs of adult learners by providing multiple paths to both nonformal and informal education. Partnerships, like the one between Iowa public libraries and ISUEO, further strengthen the lifelong learning network by providing additional resources and programming that address specific needs like financial literacy. By aligning their shared goals and drawing on their parallel histories of providing adult education outside of the boundaries of formal education, both public libraries and Cooperative Extension provide access to education to those who do not otherwise have access. Despite the challenges of a rapidly changing environment and diverse learning needs, these partnerships will widen the network of lifelong learning and strengthen learning cities.

References

Adams, H. B. (1887). *Seminary libraries and university extension*. Baltimore, MD: Johns Hopkins University. Retrieved from http://archive.org/stream/seminarylibrarie00 adamrich/seminarylibrarie00adamrich_djvu.txt

American Library Association (ALA). (1943). *Post-war standards for public libraries*. Committee on Postwar Planning. Chicago, IL: Author.

Arnot, C. A., & Eschenfelder, K. (2011, October). *Public libraries as financial literacy supporters* (2011-CFS.10). Madison: University of Wisconsin Madison Center for Financial Security.

Bliss, R. K. (1960). *History of cooperative agricultural and home economics: Extension in Iowa— The first fifty years*. Ames: Iowa State College.

Bobinski, G. S. (1969). *Carnegie libraries: Their history and impact on American public library development*. Chicago, IL: American Library Association.

Brunner, H. S. (1962). *Land-grant colleges and universities 1862–1962* (OE 50030, Bulletin 1962, No. 13). Washington, DC: U.S. Department of Health, Education, and Welfare.

Clawson, M. (2013). *New deal planning: The National Resources Planning Board*. Hoboken, NJ: Taylor and Francis. Retrieved from http://www.eblib.com

Ditzion, S. H. (1947). *Arsenals of a democratic culture*. Chicago, IL: American Library Association.

FINRA Investor Education Foundation. (2014). *About us*. Retrieved from http://www .finrafoundation.org/about/

First Morrill Act, 7 U.S.C. § 301 (1862). Retrieved from U.S. Department of Agriculture website: http://www.csrees.usda.gov/about/offices/legis/morrill.html

Gilton, D. L. (2012). *Lifelong learning in public libraries: Principles, programs, and people*. Lanham, MD: Scarecrow Press.

Hatch Act of 1887, Pub. L. No. 105-185. 2 Mar. 1887. Stat. 24.440.

Institute of Museum and Library Services (IMLS). (2009). *Museums, libraries and 21st century skills*. Washington, DC: Author.

Institute of Museum and Library Services (IMLS). (2012). *Creating a nation of learners: Strategic plan 2012–2016*. Washington, DC: Author.

Johnson, A. S. (1938). *The public library: A people's university*. New York, NY: American Association for Adult Education.

Knowles, N, S. (1920). *Annual report: Home economics*. Ames: Iowa State University Library, Special Collections.

Learned, W. S. (1924). *The American public library and the diffusion of knowledge.* New York, NY: Harcourt, Brace and Company.

Lee, R. E. (1966). *Continuing education for adults through the American public library.* Chicago, IL: American Library Association.

Leigh, R. D. (1950). *The public library in the United States.* New York, NY: Columbia University Press.

McDowell, G. R. (2001). *Land-grant universities and extension into the 21st century: Renegotiating or abandoning a social contract.* Ames: Iowa State University Press.

Monroe, M. E. (1963). *Library adult education: The biography of an idea.* New York, NY: Scarecrow Press.

Monroe, M. E., & Heim, K. M. (1991). *Partners for lifelong learning: Public libraries and adult education.* Washington, DC: Office of Library Programs, U.S. Department of Education, Office of Educational Research and Improvement.

National Association of State Universities and Land-Grant Colleges (NASULGC). (1995). *The land-grant tradition.* Washington, DC: Author.

Norman, A. C. (2012). Librarians' leadership for lifelong learning. *Public Library Quarterly, 31*(2), 91–140. doi:10.1080/01616846.2012.684577

Peich, A., & Fletcher, C. N. (2013). *Iowa Smart investing@your library® project final report.* Des Moines: Iowa Library Services.

Schweider, D. (1993). *75 years of service: Cooperative Extension in Iowa.* Ames: Iowa State University Press.

ALYSIA PEICH *is a continuing education coordinator at Iowa Library Services/State Library of Iowa.*

CYNTHIA NEEDLES FLETCHER *is a professor and an extension specialist in the Department of Human Development and Family Studies at Iowa State University.*

5

The infrastructure, financial, and human resource histories of health and education are offered as key components of future strategic planning initiatives in learning cities, and 10 key components of strategic planning initiatives designed to enhance the health and wealth of citizens of learning cities are discussed.

A Connected History of Health and Education: Learning Together Toward a Better City

Joanne Howard, Diane Howard, Ebbin Dotson

Across cities in the United States, there are similarities in the health and educational frameworks for infrastructure and organizational policies, financial and legal resources, and human resource planning. Theoretical discussions of adult learning principles and health belief model constructs also provide more insight into shared notions in the face of education and health reform for learning cities. Following an overview of education and health care, this chapter describes the health and education components of a learning city and uses 10 key components to describe how learning cities can build a strong infrastructure for health and education.

Education and Health Care: An Overview

Education and health care have been viewed as social goods provided as a right of citizenship (United Nations, 1948). As an individual gains access to social goods provided by a government, a quasi contract with that government is established. Education and health care are part of a vertical administrative pattern that is called picket-fence federalism where the lines of authority, the concerns and interests, the flow of money, and the direction of programs run straight down like a number of pickets stuck into the ground (Milakovich & Gordon, 2009).

Over the decades, education and health care have been viewed as providing the basis for economic stability and long-term growth to individuals and the country. In response to the social good that comes from having an educated and healthy populace, President Dwight D. Eisenhower established

NEW DIRECTIONS FOR ADULT AND CONTINUING EDUCATION, no. 145, Spring 2015 © 2015 Wiley Periodicals, Inc.
Published online in Wiley Online Library (wileyonlinelibrary.com) • DOI: 10.1002/ace.20123

the Department of Health, Education, and Welfare in 1953. In 1979, the Department of Education Organization Act, which officially separated education from health care, was signed into law (Graham, 2011). The Department of Education became its own cabinet post in 1980, as did health care under the Department of Health and Human Services (U.S. Department of Health and Human Services, 2011).

Education and health care are critical components of the U.S. economy, where they represent over 20% of the gross domestic product. In 2010, the United States spent $11,826 per full-time-equivalent (FTE) student on elementary and secondary education, accounting for 5.4% of GDP (World Bank Group, 2014). In 2012, $8,895 was spent per capita on health care and accounted for 17.9% of GDP (World Bank Group, 2014). Since President Eisenhower, every U.S. president has placed emphasis on the education and health of the citizenry. The difficulty each president has had is to affect change in the cost, quality, and access of these programs.

Education and health care are major initiatives that President Barack Obama has pursued since his 2008 election. At the end of 2012, the U.S. debt was $16.1 trillion (U.S. Treasury, Bureau of Fiscal Service, 2013), and states have continued to face unemployment and housing foreclosures due to the recession that appears to be abating. Both federal and state governments, as well as cities that rely on property taxes for education and health funding, are being forced to consider major budget cuts. With the budget debate becoming increasingly turbulent as 2015 comes into focus, the rationale for supporting investments in education and health care will require more thoughtful coordination. To respond to health and education reform, cities with strategic plans that include long-term strategic investments in health and education will be better positioned to engage multifaceted industry resources for this challenge.

Similarities Between Education and Health Care

Education and health care are essential services delivered by government. The idea of "America as a land of opportunity" captures an essential part of the national spirit and heritage, and public education is often viewed as the institution that can transform the ideal into reality. An equitable system of education is one that offsets those accidents of birth that would otherwise keep some children from having an opportunity to function fully in the economic and political life of the community (Berne & Stiefel, 1999). The jurisdictional issues involve not only the way schools are financed (8.3% from the federal government, with the remainder being financed by state and local governments) but also the way curriculum is developed and the accountability measures that review the performance of students, faculty, and administrators. These issues play themselves out in the media and at numerous forums and venues around the country.

Similarly, the future of our nation's health depends on equally idealistic notions. *Crossing the Quality Chasm* (Institute of Medicine, 2001), *In the*

Nation's Compelling Interest (Institute of Medicine, 2004), and *Missing Persons* (Sullivan Commission, 2004) are nationally recognized publications that contextualize the prevailing health issues of our nation. The health services research field will face future challenges related to demographic change, such as an aging workforce and an increased need for diversity (McGinnis & Moore, 2009). Racial and ethnic health disparities stemming from workforce issues will continue to intensify given the surging growth of minority populations in the United States. By 2042, one in two Americans will be an Asian American, Pacific Islander, African American, Hispanic, American Indian, and/or Alaska Native, and since 2000, Hispanics have accounted for over half of the population increase in the United States (Passell & Cohn, 2009).

Social justice research has subsumed each edge of education and health reform into a focus on health literacy. The health care arena is as prone to perpetrate injustice involving race, ethnicity, culture, poverty, immigration status, and gender as any other segment of society (Hill, 2011). In this context, a health-literate person is described as more aware of the social, economic, cultural, and environmental determinants of health, and is better prepared to engage in individual and collective actions that change those determinants (Pleasant, 2011). We will see much of these reforms play out in communities, where addressing cultural considerations, ethnic and religious diversity, and adaptations to meet ever-changing political and societal needs, community health education will become a movement for social transformation (Mayfield-Johnson, 2011; Starr, 1982).

Theory Comparison of Adult Learning and Health Behavior

In practice, there are many examples of educators working alongside people who have decided to combat the circumstances in which they live to achieve better conditions regarding environmental health and climate justice (Walter, 2007; Weinrub, 2009). Drawing connections between theoretical learning constructs of health and education will help contextualize the closeness of social justice, community health, and literacy in learning cities. As a theoretical comparison, the theories of adult learning and health behavior provide examples of how current policies and initiatives trace similar paradigms and identify components that support the learning cities movement. Adult learning is often described using learning principles (Lawler, 2003). Bryan, Kreuter, & Brownson (2009) build upon an existing Knowlesian framework of adult learning to outline five principles of adult learning:

- Adults need to know why they are learning.
- Adults are motivated to learn by the need to solve problems.
- Adults' previous experience must be respected and built upon.
- Adults need learning approaches that match their background and diversity.
- Adults need to be actively involved in the learning process.

New Directions for Adult and Continuing Education • DOI: 10.1002/ace

Comparatively, health education is often based on the constructs of the health belief model (Rosenstock, 1966, 1974). In this model, health-seeking behavior follows:

- people's beliefs about health problems,
- perceived benefits of action to seek care,
- barriers to action,
- self-efficacy,
- stimulus, or cue to action.

Together, these theories provide some insight into our current state of affairs for policy-based changes in health and education. In the historical context, programs and initiatives are often designed to address a mix of education principles or health constructs. The health belief model has been used to develop many successful health communication interventions by targeting messages at the constructs to change health behaviors (Sohl & Moyer, 2007).

In practice, resources are invested at the local level, yet these returns are measured at the state and federal levels. We are now finding research exploration in the field focusing on the leap from theory to practice, and in this context, from adult learning to health care. When blended, a host of social and nonmarket benefits are also produced, including but not limited to child well-being, health status, efficiency of consumer choices, fertility, and social capital (Montenegro & Patrinos, 2013). Hill (2011) accurately describes the current complexity that we argue will require a shared paradigm shift to solve:

> Many health care systems are increasing their expectations that patients will take responsibility for their own self- and preventive care. These demands may not intimidate the well-educated, although even they can experience difficulty because of medical information's unfamiliar vocabulary and concepts. This struggle is far more profound for poorly educated and/or low-literate individuals, immigrants learning English, and people whose cultures do not correspond with the dominant, mainstream culture commonly reproduced within health care systems. (Hill, 2011, p. 100)

Health and Education Components of a Learning City

For learning cities to thrive, we believe there are three broad dimensions of strategic planning that can be used as a conceptual framework toward a shared health and education perspective. These dimensions are described as infrastructure, financial resources, and human resources. An infrastructure, characterized in public health terms, includes the systems, competencies, frameworks, relationships, and resources that enable public health agencies to perform their core functions and essential services. Infrastructure categories encompass human, organizational, informational, legal, policy, and fiscal resources (National Association of County and City Health Officials, 2010).

New Directions for Adult and Continuing Education • DOI: 10.1002/ace

In education, the National League of Cities' Institute for Youth, Education, and Families argues, "the need for innovative financing has become even more relevant as tough budget times force cities to think strategically and systemically about supporting the [educational] options available in their communities" (Russell, 2009, p. 1). Although national government support is available, they are primarily the financial responsibility of the individual city concerned. Hence, the strategic impact (long term, or regional and national) tends to be lower on the policy agenda, with the main emphasis placed on short-term and local concerns (Pratt, 2010).

The human resource arena includes discussions of integrated and transparent governance, strategic and promotional activities, networking, and partnerships (Odendaal, 2003). Florida states that a strategic plan for human resources includes coordination between creative occupations and workforce, knowledge networks, voluntary organizations, crime-free environments, and even the after-dark entertainment economy as a crucial axis for city development (Florida, 2002). A strong educational system is a critical magnet that makes a city attractive in which businesses, organizations, and individuals of all backgrounds gravitate to dynamic learning environments (Nam & Pardo, 2011).

Here, we provide 10 components of the three dimensions that, together, inform the nation on the future direction of the impact that learning cities momentum can have on better health and education.

Building an Infrastructure.

1. *Historical facts that create paralysis.* Education and health care are essential services delivered by government. The idea of "America as a land of opportunity" captures an essential part of the national spirit and heritage, and public education is often viewed as the institution that can transform the ideal into reality. An equitable system of education is one that offsets those accidents of birth that would otherwise keep some children from having an opportunity to function fully in the economic and political life of the community (Berne & Stiefel, 1999).

   The introduction of Medicare and Medicaid for the aged and poor, respectively, in 1965 was the major hallmark of health care reform in the 20th century. Small, incremental changes have made health care a patchwork of programs and services where its financing and payment controls are the mechanism to allow patients to get access to services. One in every seven U.S. dollars is devoted to health care (Cutler, 2008) and so its sheer size has gotten difficult to control. The patchwork of remedies over the years has added to its complexity and dissatisfaction of patients who have to access it.

   Implication for learning cities. Lack of organizational cohesion and political environment can hinder infrastructure development.
2. *Threat from international systems that invest in education and public health.* The United States finds itself in a global community where competition

between countries that invest in education has become fierce. The World Bank (Montenegro & Patrinos, 2013) reported that the average rate of return to another year of schooling is 10% with the average return to schooling being the highest in Latin America and the Caribbean region and for the Sub-Saharan Africa region. The research also indicates that as education increases, personal income increases. The same can be said for health.

For education, the Program for International Student Assessment (PISA) tests were announced on December 7, 2010 by the Organization for Economic Co-operation and Development (OECD). PISA provides a detailed assessment and comparison of what 15-year-old students in 74 education systems have learned and how well they can apply their knowledge (Paine & Schleicher, 2011). PISA results for U.S. students fell around the OECD average range, as they have for the past decade, with scores around the average for reading and science and below average in mathematics (Paine & Schleicher, 2011). Recent top performers—nations as diverse as South Korea, Finland, Canada, The Netherlands, and Japan—continued to rank among the top 10 in combined average scores.

Health care costs have skyrocketed in the United States to the extent that patients are flying abroad to receive care. This phenomenon (called "medical tourism") is challenging the way tertiary hospitals and physicians do business. In 2007, between 50,300 and 121,400 people from other countries traveled into the United States, and between 42,600 and 102,900 Americans traveled outside the United States for medical care that required an inpatient hospital stay (Johnson & Garman, 2010). Since 1980, the United States has had the highest average annual growth rates in per capita spending on health care. Despite this relatively high level of spending, the United States does not provide substantially greater health resources to its citizens, or achieve substantially better health benchmarks, compared to other developed countries (Kaiser Snapshots, 2011).

Implication for learning cities. The competing authorities (federal, state, and local) can complicate goal setting and resource sharing.

3. *Management of education and health care.* The management of education systems has been the provenance of doctoral prepared educators (EdD or PhD) for many years. However, in the past 15 years the landscape has been altered (Clifford & Guthrie, 1990). The recent criticism of principal and teacher preparation programs has resulted in the pipeline to a superintendent position, the most senior position in a district or state, going to people with an orientation other than education. Urban districts such as New York, Chicago, and Los Angeles have selected leaders with backgrounds in publishing, finance, former elected officials, and law. The second person in charge has routinely been the chief academic officer or a person with classroom and curriculum experience (Clifford & Guthrie, 1990). Improving the learning for school-age children, given these new

changes in the management and leadership of education, will need to be further examined.

The management of health care organizations had traditionally been the purview of graduates of master's programs in health administration and public health. There are over 140 undergraduate and graduate programs in health administration in the country (Association of University Programs in Health Administration, 2010). The complexity of health care with the growing emphasis on accounting and finance in the 1990s moved many business schools to start health care specialties. The influx of business school graduates and the industry need to attract business-oriented managers have changed the character of the health management field from a patient-centered, public good orientation to that of a business, commodity orientation (Howard, 2005). The expansion of an organization's infrastructure, research, and technology and the finances needed to sustain the profitability of the enterprise require business skills to manage.

Implication for learning cities. Political and social "will" often direct accountability and central management decisions.

Building Financial Resources.

4. *Perceived value of education and health care.* In the 1944 State of the Union to Congress, Franklin Delano Roosevelt discussed a second Bill of Rights that included the rights to work, food, clothing, recreation, housing, economic security, and education. In 1941, President Roosevelt delivered a speech where he declared "freedom from want" as one of four essential liberties to achieve human security. The right to adequate medical care and the opportunity to achieve and enjoy good health was included in his definition of human security (Carmalt & Zaidi, 2004).

In 1948, the United Nations adopted the Universal Declaration of Human Rights, where "everyone has the right to a standard of living adequate for the health and well-being of oneself and one's family, including food, clothing, housing, and medical care" (United Nations, 1948, Article 25). The United Nations through the World Health Organization declared that vulnerability to ill health can be reduced by taking steps to respect the rights to food and nutrition, water, education, and adequate housing (United Nations, 1948). The linkage between health and education was embodied by these 1940s pronouncements during and after World War II.

Conservative critics of school finance reform state that money does not matter in the education of a child. But visitors to public schools throughout the country understand that money may not be the entire story, but that it does indeed matter. What does better school funding provide for a child? First, it pays for a building that provides space for each child to grow and learn, which is outfitted with amenities (air conditioning, adequate lighting and heating plant, video and audio capability, cafeteria that serves healthy food, a library that not only has books but books that are current and relevant, the building is clean and has a security detail and sufficient parking for faculty and staff) that allow learning to take root. Money also pays teachers who are highly competent and an administrative staff that provides them with the support they need to get the job done. Money also buys the extras—outfitted labs, choir, arts, cultural exchanges, sports teams with coaches, and the ability to attract more talent and resources. In these schools, success breeds continued success with a strong curriculum, parental and community involvement, and a school culture that encourages excellence and advances in learning.

Good health, comparable to a good education, is an ideal. It is something that people who have been born with good health generally take for granted. It is not until a personal or family health episode that U.S. citizens start to perceive health as a priority. The perceived value of health care gets diluted by the many issues in health care delivery and financing. In recent years, concerns have been centered on insurance coverage for pharmaceuticals, the reorganization of Medicare and Medicaid, and quality reporting. The perception of health care delivery and financing varies by race/ethnicity and income (Kaiser Health Security Watch, 2011). The more educated and financially stable view the health care system as functioning well with minor areas for improvement, while racial and ethnic minorities and those with low income remain worried about health care–related issues and medical spending (Kaiser Health Security Watch, 2011).

Implication for learning cities. Equitable distribution of resources is a broader (regional or state) problem.

5. *Cost and quality.* The education cost per pupil expenditures (PPE) adjusted for regional cost differences is $11,223 (Hightower, 2011) in the United States. The education cost per pupil expenditures in Finland, the school system most often mentioned as ideal, is less than $8,000 per year. Theory has it that the reason Finnish schools have better outcomes is the country is smaller, the population is more homogeneous, there is less income inequality, and the family structure (smaller families) provides fewer hardships for children during economic downturns. There is also considerably less bureaucracy in Finland when it comes to education. The United States has multiple levels of bureaucracy that are not always aligned.

In a Commonwealth Fund publication, Davis, Schoen, and Stremlkis (2010) reported that, despite having the most expensive health care system, the United States ranks last overall compared to six other industrialized countries—Australia, Canada, Germany, the Netherlands, New Zealand, and the United Kingdom—on measures of health system performance in five areas: quality, efficiency, access to care, equity, and the ability to lead long, healthy, and productive lives. While there is room for improvement in every country, the United States stands out for not getting good value for its health care dollars, ranking last despite spending $8,895 per capita on health care in 2012 compared to the $5,737 spent per capita in the Netherlands, which ranked first overall (World Bank Group, 2014).

Implication for learning cities: A well-defined unit of measurement will help to address cost, quality, and equitable distribution issues.

6. *Challenges to traditional organization structure.* Profit-making education companies attempt to respond to parental demand for more choice so the states have created charter schools, which are typically started by groups of parents and teachers (Symonds, Palmer, Lindorff, & McCann, 2000). The application for a charter is usually issued by a school board, university, or state agency to receive tax dollars, but the school may operate independently of the rules that govern most public schools (Symonds et al., 2000). Minnesota passed the first charter-school law in 1990, and the concept has now spread to 40 states, Puerto Rico, and the District of Columbia. In December 2000, *Business Week* reported that the National Education Goals conceded that the United States had fallen far short of the aims governors had set a decade ago (Rothman, 2000). The percent of students earning a standard diploma in four years shifted from 69.2% in 2006 to 68.8% in 2007, and U.S. 12th graders came in 15th out of 20 developed countries on international math tests and 12th in science (Rothman, 2000).

The Depression brought about losses in the for-profit hospital sector because of its small business orientation. The physician owners of for-profit hospitals went to work for their former competitors in the nonprofit sector (Needleman, 1999). The infusion of capital through the Hill–Burton program caused the explosion of the nonprofit hospital sector with capital improvement support that was not available to the for-profit sector.

Implication for learning cities. Larger cities often have more resources to utilize, but also more complexities to manage, more variability in needs, and more vested interests to take into account with resources.

7. *Rural–urban issues.* While many believe urban school districts receive limited resources from many state governments, rural school districts are also underfinanced because there are fewer sources of revenue to support these schools. For example, the state of New Jersey had protracted school reform issues before their state supreme court (*Robinson v. Cahill* and *Abbott v. Burke*). *Abbott* went through 21 iterations, and with each state court ruling, additional resources were deemed appropriate for urban school districts. Rural district wishing to take advantage of additional financial support from the State of New Jersey became a part of the *Abbott* case and, as a result of the remedies mandated by the court, received additional resources. The State of New Jersey now has 31 school districts labeled as *Abbott* districts. Three of these districts are in rural areas of the state (Howard, 2006).

Health care has a comparable urban–suburban–rural dynamic. The urban centers are affected by the social and economic climate of a city, be it positive or negative. Traditionally, academic medical centers have been located in urban areas near public transportation routes where they provide the most sophisticated level of care (e.g., transplants and trauma services; Guagliardo, 2004). The academic medical centers and most urban hospitals will struggle to provide services by a patient's insurance classification, particularly to a Medicare, Medicaid, and self-pay population (American Hospital Association, 2011). Lacking a diversity of payer classes that include a larger percentage of commercial payers who reimburse at a higher percentage of medical and administrative costs, these urban centers can become financially challenged. The suburban hospital may fare better financially because its clientele will be commercially insured. The rural hospital will struggle with limited resources due to a smaller population base with the same payer mix issues as the urban hospital (National Rural Health Association, 2013).

Implication for learning cities. Counties often serve as bridging agencies between districts. Cohesion is important for sustainable growth and success.

Building Human Resources.

8. *Business demanding reforms.* The United States was the first country to offer every young person the opportunity to obtain a free public secondary education at the end of the 19th and beginning of the 20th century and reaped tremendous economic rewards for doing so. The major shift in secondary education occurred after 1910 where it was transformed into "training for life" rather than college (Goldin & Katz, 1999, p. 689). Through public funding, by 1910, 49% of high school graduates continued to some form of higher education (Goldin & Katz, 1999). The United States also led the world in the number of postsecondary college and university degrees after World War II when the G.I. bill made it possible for thousands of returning veterans to attend school. The large cohort of U.S. Baby Boomers began going on to college and by the end of the 1970s a college degree was viewed by most people in the United States as the single most important factor in obtaining a good job and an economically secure life (Paine & Schleicher, 2011).

A group of large companies came together in 1998 to discuss how they could impact the safety, quality, and affordability of health care. With the Institute of Medicine (1999) report that advocated reducing medical errors and enhancing patient safety, the Leapfrog Group was formed. This voluntary organization of employers liaises with the Centers for Medicare and Medicaid, the U.S. Office of Personnel Management, the Department of Defense, and the Minnesota Department of Human Services and Employee Relations. Leapfrog has initiatives in developing data sets that will allow the public to compare the performance of hospitals, health plans, and clinical teams that will appear on the organization's website (Galvin, Delbanco, Milstein, & Belden, 2005). The demand by large corporations to reduce health care costs has reached a peak. Another aspect of the Accountable Care Organization is a federal initiative to move physicians, hospitals, and ancillary providers to develop medical homes and better coordinate care thus reducing health care costs.

Implication for learning cities. Create and strengthen partnerships with field- and industry-leading organizations, especially those with hiring capacity.

9. *Student/patient outcomes.* The publication of *A Nation at Risk* in 1983 made Americans more aware and increasingly concerned about the quality of education. U.S. academic performance had slipped, and a sharp drop-off in average scholastic aptitude test (SAT) scores between 1963 and 1979 gave evidence of a decline in American educational standards. While performance on these tests has improved, there continues to be a concern about educational outcomes in the country (Burtless, 1996).

Criticism in health care has revolved around costs and patient outcomes.

The Institute of Medicine reports *To Err is Human* (1999) and *Crossing the Quality Chasm* (2001) brought attention to medical error, patient safety, and clinical outcomes. Since these landmark reports, the Department of Health and Human Services, the Joint Commission, hospitals, and health care providers have devoted considerable time and attention to improve the patient experience and eliminate patient harm (Institute of Medicine, 1999, 2001).

Pay for performance or "P4P" was initiated following the Institute of Medicine publication *Crossing the Quality Chasm* (2001) that discussed unintended deaths in health care and a different focus on delivering quality measures and cost savings (Baker & Carter, 2004). While commercial insurance companies had been experimenting with this cost-saving philosophy and programs for years, the federal government's adoption of such strategies has intensified the focus on patient outcomes by reducing clinical variation and errors, and using measures that assess the appropriateness of hospital and emergency department visits and transparency of providers' performance (Baker, 2003).

Implication for learning cities. For educational and clinical outcomes to be impactful, they should affect multiple communities and neighborhoods.

10. *Staff shortages.* Over 50% of the nation's teachers and principals are baby boomers (Aaronson & Meckel, 2008). During the next four years, the United States could lose one third of its most accomplished educators to retirement. The wave of departures peaked during the 2010–2011 school year, when over 100,000 veteran teachers could have retired. In less than a decade, more than half of today's teachers—1.7 million—could be gone

(Carroll & Foster, 2008). The retirement situation is exacerbated by the number of rookie teachers that leave the profession within five years of their arrival (Carroll & Foster, 2008).

Individuals known as baby boomers have started to retire; these retirements will also exacerbate the nurse and physician supply issues. By 2025, there will be a shortage of 300,000 nurses and 35,000 to 40,000 primary care physicians (Cooper et al., 2009). The influx of patients from the Patient Protection and Affordable Care Act of 2010 will further complicate the supply issue.

Implication for learning cities. A targeted recruitment plan is the first step in addressing industry shortages. Growing fields will need more marketing support.

Discussion/Conclusion

In this chapter, we have tried to contextualize an idea posed by Lillian Hill into the learning cities discussion. Her idea that adult educators are key to public health success can be applied to learning cities. If learning is central to health, and not enough providers have the training to discern when low literacy, poverty, and differing health beliefs and practices are present in the health care encounter, they will not be as effective as they could be if they collaborated with adult educators, whose insights regarding adult learning are critical in helping adults learn about their disease states and appropriate actions they could take (Hill, 2011). If the learning cities concept is considered a modern day movement to enhance adult learning and literacy through such practices as community engagement and public advocacy, education and health care can be thought of as a blueprint for reforming key services for communities.

Schools and hospitals serve as the center of education and health care because they each bring students and patients, respectively, into organizational structures. The loci of adult students and patients make it more efficient for learning and the provision of care. With the growing U.S. federal and state deficits, there are considerations being given to reduce the deficits by terminating supports to traditional education and health care. Prior to making such decisions, there needs to be an examination of the social contract that government has with its citizens. Education and health care are two of those contracts. It would be prudent to examine the history of these contracts before limiting their support. For cities with strategic goals to invest in one or the other, this discussion includes components that are essential building blocks for change.

References

Aaronson, D., & Meckel, K. (2008, September). The impact of baby boomer retirements on teacher labor markets. *The Federal Reserve Bank of Chicago, 254.* Retrieved from ERIC database: http://files.eric.ed.gov/fulltext/ED505644.pdf

American Hospital Association. (2011). *Trendwatch: The opportunities and challenges for rural hospitals in an era of health reform.* Retrieved from http://www.aha.org/research /reports/tw/11apr-tw-rural.pdf

Association of University Programs in Health Administration. (2010). *Health administration programs.* Retrieved from http://www.aupha.org/resourcecenter

Baker, G. (2003). *Pay for performance incentive programs in healthcare: Market dynamics and business process.* San Francisco, CA: MedVantage.

Baker, G., & Carter, B. (2004). *The evolution of pay for performance models for rewarding providers: Case studies in health plan pay for performance.* Washington, DC: Atlantic Information Services.

Berne, R., & Stiefel, L. (1999). Concepts of school finance equity: 1970 to present. In H. F. Ladd (Ed.), *Equity and adequacy in education finance: Issues and perspectives* (pp. 7–33). Washington, DC: National Academy Press.

Bryan R. L., Kreuter, M. W., & Brownson, R. C. (2009). Integrating adult learning principles into training for public health practice. *Health Promotion Practice, 10,* 557–563.

Burtless, G. (1996). *Does money matter?: The effect of school resources on student achievement and adult success.* Washington, DC: The Brookings Institution.

Carmalt, J., & Zaidi, S. (2004). *The right to health in the United States of America: What does it mean?* Washington, DC: Center for Economic and Social Rights.

Carroll, T. G., & Foster, E. (2008). *Learning teams: Creating what's next.* Washington, DC: National Commission on Teaching America's Future.

Clifford, G. J., & Guthrie, J. W. (1990). *Ed school: A brief for professional education.* Chicago, IL: University of Chicago.

Cooper, R. A., Getzen, T., Johns, M. M., Ross-Lee, B., Sheldon, G. F., & Whitcomb, M. E. (2009). *Physicians and their practices under health care reform: A report to the President and the Congress.* Boston, MA: The Physicians Foundation.

Cutler, D. M. (2008, May). The American healthcare system. *Medical solutions.* Retrieved from www.siemens.com/healthcare-magazine

Davis, K., Schoen, C., & Stremlkis, K. (2010, June). *Mirror, mirror on the wall: How the performance of the U.S. healthcare system compares internationally.* New York, NY: The Commonwealth Fund.

Florida, R. (2002). *The rise of the creative class: And how it's transforming work, leisure, community and everyday life.* New York, NY: Basic Books.

Galvin, R. S., Delbanco, S., Milstein, A., & Belden, G. (2005). Has the Leapfrog Group had an impact on the health care market? *Health Affairs, 24*(1), 228–233.

Goldin, C., & Katz, L. (1999). Human capital and social capital: The rise of secondary schooling in America, 1910–1940. *Journal of Interdisciplinary History, 29,* 683–723.

Graham, H. D. (2011). *The uncertain triumph: Federal education policy in the Kennedy and Johnson years.* Chapel Hill: University of North Carolina Press.

Guagliardo, M. F. (2004). Spatial accessibility of primary care: Concepts, methods and challenges. *International Journal of Health Geographics, 3*(3), 1–13. Retrieved from http://www.ij-healthgeographics.com/content/pdf/1476-072X-3-3.pdf

Hightower, A. (2011, January). State performance and policymaking: Weighing in, measuring up, quality counts. *Education Week.* Retrieved from http://www.edweek.org/ew /articles/2011/01/13/16stateofthestates.h30.html?intc=ml

Hill, L. H. (2011). Health education as an arena for adult educators' engagement in social justice. In L. H. Hill (Ed.), *New Directions for Adult and Continuing Education: No. 130. Adult education for health and wellness* (pp. 99–104). San Francisco, CA: Jossey-Bass.

Howard, D. (2005). *Blue Cross Blue Shield conversions and the impact on individual product offerings.* Ann Arbor, MI: UMI Dissertation Services.

Howard, J. E. (2006). *Abbott v. Burke: An historical analysis of school finance reform in New Jersey.* Ann Arbor, MI: UMI Dissertation Services.

Institute of Medicine. (1999). *To err is human.* Washington, DC: National Academy Press.

Institute of Medicine. (2001). *Crossing the quality chasm: A new health system for the 21st Century*. Washington, DC: National Academy Press.

Institute of Medicine. (2004). *In the nation's compelling interest: Ensuring diversity in the health care workforce*. Washington, DC: National Academy Press.

Johnson, T. J., & Garman, A. N. (2010). Impact of medical travel on imports and exports of medical services. *Health Policy, 98*(2–3), 171–177.

Kaiser Health Security Watch. (2011). *Kaiser public opinion*. Retrieved from www.kff.org

Kaiser Snapshots. (2011). *Health care spending in the United States and selected OECD countries*. Retrieved from http://kff.org/health-costs/issue-brief/snapshots-health-care-spending-in-the-united-states-selected-oecd-countries/

Lawler, P. (2003). Teachers as adult learners: A new perspective. In K. P. King & P. A. Lawler (Eds.), *New Directions for Adult and Continuing Education: No. 98. Perspectives on designing and implementing professional development of teachers of adults* (pp. 15–22). San Francisco, CA: Jossey-Bass.

Mayfield-Johnson, S. (2011). Adult learning, community education, and public health: Making the connection through community health advisors. In L. H. Hill (Ed.), *New Directions for Adult and Continuing Education: No. 130. Adult education for health and wellness* (pp. 65–77). San Francisco, CA: Jossey-Bass.

McGinnis, S., & Moore, J. (2009). The health services research workforce: Current stock. *Health Services Research, 44*, 2214–2226.

Milakovich, M. E., & Gordon, G. J. (2009). *Public administration in America* (10th ed.). Boston, MA: Wadsworth Cengage Learning.

Montenegro, C., & Patrinos, H. (2013). *Returns to schooling around the world* [Background paper for the World Development Report 2013]. Washington, DC: World Bank.

Nam, T., & Pardo, T. A. (2011, June). *Conceptualizing smart city with dimensions of technology, people, and institutions*. Proceedings of the 12th Annual International Digital Government Research Conference: Digital Government Innovation in Challenging Times, University of Maryland College Park, College Park.

National Association of County and City Health Officials (NACCHO). (2010). *Developing a local health department strategic plan: A how-to-guide*. Retrieved from http://www.naccho.org/topics/infrastructure/accreditation/upload/StrategicPlanningGuideFinal.pdf

National Rural Health Association. (2013). *The future of rural health*. Retrieved from http://www.ruralhealthweb.org/index.cfm?objectid=EAB2AE78-3048-651A-FE4CBFB6C083F34F

Needleman, J. (1999). Nonprofit to for-profit conversions by hospitals, health insurers, and health plans. *Public Health Reports, 114*, 108–119.

Odendaal, N. (2003). Information and communication technology and local governance: Understanding the difference between cities in developed and emerging economies. *Computers, Environment and Urban Systems, 27*(6), 585–607.

Paine, S. L., & Schleicher, A. (2011). *What the U.S. can learn from the world's most successful education reform efforts*. New York, NY: McGraw-Hill Research Foundation.

Passell, J., & Cohn, D. (2009). A portrait of unauthorized immigrants in the United States. *Pew Hispanic Center*. Retrieved from http://pewhispanic.org/files/reports/107.pdf

Pleasant, A. (2011). Health literacy: An opportunity to improve individual, community, and global health. In L. H. Hill (Ed.), *New Directions for Adult and Continuing Education: No. 130. Adult education for health and wellness* (pp. 43–53). San Francisco, CA: Jossey-Bass.

Pratt, A. C. (2010). Creative cities: Tensions within and between social, cultural and economic development. A critical reading of the UK experience. *City, Culture and Society, 1*(1), 13–20.

Rosenstock, I. M. (1966). Why people use health services. *The Milbank Memorial Fund Quarterly, 44*(3), 94–127.

Rosenstock, I. M. (1974). Historical origins of the health belief model. *Health Education & Behavior, 2*(4), 328–335.

Rothman, R. (2000). *Bringing all students to high standards: Report on National Education Goals Panel, Field Hearings*. Retrieved from http://govinfo.library.unt.edu/negp/issues/publication/negpdocs/negprep/rpt_fldhrng/fldhrng.pdf

Russell, L. (2009). *Financial strategies to support citywide systems of out-of-school time programs*. Retrieved from http://www.wallacefoundation.org/knowledge-center/after-school/coordinating-after-school-resources/Documents/Financial-Strategies-to-Support-Citywide-Systems-of-Out-of-School-Time-Programs.pdf

Sohl, S. J., & Moyer, A. (2007). Tailored interventions to promote mammography screening: A meta-analytic review. *Preventative Medicine, 45*, 252–261.

Starr, P. (1982). *The social transformation of American medicine: The rise of a sovereign profession and the making of a vast industry*. New York, NY: Basic Books.

Sullivan Commission. (2004). *Missing persons: Minorities in the health professions: A report of the Sullivan Commission on Diversity in the Healthcare Workforce*. Retrieved from http://www.aacn.nche.edu/Media/pdf/SullivanReport.pdf

Symonds, W. C., Palmer, T., Lindorff, D., & McCann, J. (2000, February). For-profit schools: They're spreading fast. Can private companies do a better job of educating America's kids? *BusinessWeek*. Retrieved from http://www.businessweek.com/2000/00_06/b3667001.htm

United Nations. (1948). *The universal declaration of human rights*. Retrieved from http://www.un.org/en/documents/udhr/

U.S. Department of Health and Human Services. (2011). *Historical highlights*. Retrieved from http://www.hhs.gov/about/hhshist.html

U.S. Treasury, Bureau of Fiscal Service. (2013). *Historical debt outstanding: Annual 2000–2012*. Retrieved from http://www.treasurydirect.gov/govt/reports/pd/histdebt/histdebt_histo5.htm

Walter, P. (2007). Adult learning in new social movements: Environmental protest and the struggle for the Clayoquot Sound rainforest. *Adult Education Quarterly, 57*(3), 248–263.

Weinrub, A. (2009). Oakland Coalition charts new course on climate strategy. *Race, Poverty & the Environment, 16*, 28–31.

World Bank Group. (2014). *United States*. Retrieved from http://data.worldbank.org/country/united-states

JOANNE HOWARD *is an assistant professor in public administration and associate of the Educational Leadership Program in the College of Education at Roosevelt University–Chicago.*

DIANE HOWARD *is an assistant professor in the Department of Health Systems Management and director of Student Development at Rush University–Chicago.*

EBBIN DOTSON *is an assistant professor in the Division of Community Health Sciences and assistant dean for the Office of Diversity and Inclusion at the University of Illinois at Chicago–School of Public Health.*

6

This chapter considers leisure as a powerful agent for social change alongside the field of adult education in bringing to life the idea of learning cities.

Role of Leisure in Humanizing Learning Cities

Dan K. Hibbler, Leodis Scott

Over the past 50 years, in an effort to validate the vital research on leisure behavior, leisure scholars have worked vigorously to define and establish leisure studies as a legitimate field of scholarship and professional practice. Although leisure scholars have made significant progress, most people continue to think of leisure merely as recreational activities when away from work. While there is nothing erroneous about this view, leisure seen solely as recreation actually limits its broad disciplinary scope and societal impact. In this chapter, we consider leisure as a powerful agent for social change as well as having a role in working alongside the adult education field in bringing to life the idea of learning cities. Leisure scholarship, history, and practice have the potential to transform the way we live by centering education on learners and their communities, improving our overall health and well-being, and even "humanizing" our cities into places for continued learning, education, experience, and engagement.

In this chapter, we intend to explore multiple definitions of leisure, its ancient history, and recent scholarship that promote leisure education, social networks, and lifelong learning. Few scholars have addressed or advanced the need for lifelong learning that Verduin and McEwen (1984) encouraged that connects adult learners to leisure and combines both fields of leisure studies and adult and continuing education. We will discuss the basic points about how leisure helps advance the idea of learning cities and will show the social and personal impact of leisure on adult learners.

What Is Leisure?

The word *leisure* has multiple meanings and responses particularly in scholarly circles of adult, higher, and continuing education. Wide disparity remains in

NEW DIRECTIONS FOR ADULT AND CONTINUING EDUCATION, no. 145, Spring 2015 © 2015 Wiley Periodicals, Inc.
Published online in Wiley Online Library (wileyonlinelibrary.com) • DOI: 10.1002/ace.20124

ongoing professional work, service administration, and consultation regarding leisure and its definition. Arguably, leisure is one of those highly disputed terms, similar to love, culture, race, or even who is the best athlete, most famous sports team, or all other popular thoughts in American culture and society. Leisure has different meanings for different individuals and groups. The meanings of leisure and their associated actions can also change over time and be dependent on situation, context, or environment.

Leisure scholars and theorists have agreed upon a set of topics that define leisure as either time, activity, or state of mind (Godbey, 2003; Kraus, 1994, 2000; Sharma, 1990; Stokowski, 1994), and as a group of values such as enjoyment, happiness, satisfaction, or creativity for physical, mental, social development, interaction, and participation (Dumazedier, 1974; Verduin & McEwen, 1984). Leisure has a long history from ancient cultures in Africa, Greece, Rome, and China. Perspectives from these ancient cultures help to inform our American topics and values of leisure, including being a symbol of social class (Veblen, 1899), which has led more recent scholars to consider the social agency of leisure. In fact, Kelly (2012) suggests that leisure is "experience, decision, development, identity, interaction, institutional, political, and human" (p. 494). These combinations of views, topics, and values can help to define leisure as a hybrid of perspectives that indicate the personal and social importance of leisure, especially in our discussion about adult education and learning cities.

Historical Influences of Leisure

The historical influences of leisure help to describe how we see leisure today. For the purposes of this chapter, we can also borrow many ideas about how leisure contributed to entire societies and cultures. With the overall idea of learning cities (the main theme of this volume), leisure plays an important role in the personal and social construction of individuals that will inform, entertain, and enlighten for the good of all.

Africa: Birthplace of Leisure Culture. It is not completely clear what role leisure played in the lives of early humans. However, archaeologists have found evidence of leisure culture in ancient civilizations. Africa, the birthplace of the human race, may also be the birthplace of leisure culture. Archeologists have identified an African community—the Kingdom of Kush—that arose around 4,000 BC (Bayley, Baynes, & Kendall, 2004; Russell, 2009). The archaeological findings determined that the Kushites engaged in primitive leisure with an emphasis on teaching community members how to survive in the rough landscape adjacent to Egypt. Like the Egyptians, the Kushites were fascinated by body adornment including primitive tattoos, makeup, hairpieces, oils, and scents along with extravagant clothing for festive occasions (Russell, 2009). There is much conjecture about how people in ancient culture spent their leisure time, but there seems to be some agreement that much of leisure was used for teaching, learning, and celebrating.

New Directions for Adult and Continuing Education • DOI: 10.1002/ace

Ancient Greece: Intellectual and Physical Nature of Leisure. It was clear that the ancient Greeks were in constant search for the good life and leisure was the direct path to such endeavor (Sylvester, 1999). Ancient Greek philosophers, namely Socrates, Plato, and Aristotle, represented a larger culture that considered the value of contemplation in examining the nature of life as a proper use of leisure. Schools such as Plato's *Academy* and Aristotle's *Lyceum* serve as examples of having discussions and lectures about life that today would be associated with more leisurely and academic pursuits. In fact, the word leisure is derived from the Greek word *schole*, which also includes an idea of a school, or a place where leisure pursuits are embraced (Russell, 2013). As such, one of the common threads throughout Ancient Greece was that leisure pursuits held a dual nature, both intellectual and physical (Russell, 2009). The legacy of the leisure culture of Ancient Greece is strong in American culture; it is evident in theatrical plays and epic poems that were produced to entertain and educate, in the beauty of the art and architecture, and in the excitement of sports and gaming. The ancient Greeks were the founders of the Olympic games and physical contests for the worship of the gods (Russell, 2013). Through the historical influence of Ancient Greece, we see how leisure culture brought together learning, physical activity, and religious ritual for the benefit of society.

Ancient Rome: Leisure for Social Control. The Ancient Romans were excellent record keepers, builders, and promoters of leisure. Like many today, the Romans divided their time between work and leisure; they enjoyed many of the same leisure activities that many enjoy today, such as swimming, running, fishing, and games (Fife, 2012). However, Romans are remembered in history for the large-scale, mass leisure they staged; much has been written by historians and performed in motion pictures sensationalizing the gladiators, chariot races, and other physical contests that characterized the barbaric Roman era of leisure.

As Rome conquered its neighbors Greece, Syria, Egypt, Macedonia, and others, the empire assimilated many different groups of people under one rule and one social order (Russell, 2013). Controlling the masses and the growing middle class became a high priority for the ruling class. The Romans were among the first culture that we know of to have used leisure as a form of social control (Kraus, 2000). Gigantic amphitheaters were constructed and the citizens of Rome were entertained at large-scale, elaborate events attended during public holidays in these spaces. At the Colosseum, up to 80,000 Romans could gather to watch gladiators fight to the death. The spectacles illustrate the publicized relationship of leisure and government using circuses, pageants, festivals, and other large displays by totalitarian rulers for distracting their people from more important issues and concerns (Kaplan, 1960, 1975). The purpose was to entertain and subdue the masses while at the same time alerting all citizens about the power of the ruling class.

Today, leisure for the masses is a part of community life. Public events like concerts, professional games, plays in open-air venues, and movies in the park are just a few examples of mass leisure that can entertain and enlighten, and also where individuals together can begin to develop social networks and experience a sense of belonging. Large public events that provide leisure and recreational outlets, while not directly considering their social control or societal impact, have garnered a generally positive influence on individuals and communities.

Early China: Leisure for Life Balance and Lifelong Learning. Much of early Chinese leisure and related literature have wide influence from the teachings of the philosopher Confucius. Confucius taught lessons related to peace, order, harmony, calmness, and life balance. The early Chinese society had a passion for using leisure as a teaching method; it wanted its citizens to have an appreciation for the literary and martial arts (Ibrahim, 1991). Later, the Tang Dynasty (618–907) was very interested in transforming China into a successful cosmopolitan society that included music, literature, and visual arts (Tregear, 1985). The early Chinese were very committed to learning through leisure. The commitment can be understood through their architecture. Each building was designed to render something special such as for admiring the moonlight, making paintings, and composing music (Russell, 2009). The early Chinese made a commitment to life balance and learning through their leisure pursuits.

Historic America: Leisure for the Wealthy Social Class. Thorstein Veblen, an American economist and sociologist, produced writings in the late 19th century that were the catalyst for viewing leisure as a symbol of social status. In his seminal work, *The Theory of the Leisure Class*, Veblen was critical of the upper class and labeled them as the "idle rich" and "exploiters" who lived off the toil of others (Veblen, 1899). Veblen coined the phrase "conspicuous consumption" to describe the habits of the wealthy in the late 19th and early 20th century (pp. 68–69). Some might argue that conspicuous consumption has become a way of life in the United States. Decadent lifestyles are on display every day in films, on reality television shows, in pop songs, and in social media. Conspicuous consumption is no longer the provenance of the rich, as the case that Veblen first described, but now is prevalent among all classes. It has become commonplace for many to put themselves into debt to live a lifestyle that is the envy of their friends and neighbors.

In a famous essay *In Praise of Idleness*, Bertrand Russell, a British philosopher, expressed that it has always been shocking to the rich that the poor should have leisure (Russell, 1935/1960). As Russell concedes, "the wise use of leisure . . . is a product of civilization and education" (pp. 14–15). Unfortunately, consumption of all kinds has been widely associated and confused with leisure behavior. Yet through leisure education, individuals of all socioeconomic classes can learn to become effective and healthy consumers of leisure. Within cities and communities, leisure can become equitable and inclusive and can serve the needs of all people, irrespective of work and economic status.

Industrial Revolution as Most Significant Influence on Leisure. In further describing the historical influences on leisure, the Industrial

Revolution has been marked as the most significant (Stokowski, 1994). The Industrial Revolution, beginning in the 1870s, transformed relationships between people. As such, Kraus (1971) notes several relational effects, namely that it created new urban societies, established an industrial lifestyle, strengthened a work ethic, and encouraged recreation as time "left over" after work. In addition, during the Industrial Revolution in Britain and later in the United States, land for public parks and recreation areas were set aside. During this same time, universities across the United States began academic leisure studies programs to combat the social problems associated with the Industrial Revolution (Kraus, 1971; Stokowski, 1994).

Stokowski (1994) believes that the Industrial Revolution "reinforced the separation of leisure and work" and how people must define their life (either good or bad) in relation to their work and production (pp. 6–7). This separation, Stokowski proposes, has led to the confusion between "work-like" leisure and "leisure-like" work (p. 7). An example of work-like leisure may be so-called DIY (do-it-yourself) activities, such as home-building projects performed during nonwork hours (without compensation), but designed to increase the value of your home. On the other hand, an example of leisure-like work can be seen as those employed as lifeguards who also love swimming, music instructors who love music, or other professionals (maybe even certain leisure scholars and adult educators) who see their real work not really as work, but as creative opportunities in living more fulfilled lives.

In addition, the Industrial Revolution marked a period in history when modern recreation and leisure programming as we know it today were established (Kaplan, 1960). For example, in 1889, Jane Addams and Ellen Gates Starr opened Hull House with their own funding in a dilapidated, donated house in Chicago (McBride, 1989). Hull House, the first of its kind, became a recreation center with a day care center. Classes and clubs were established for teens, and adult education programs served immigrants and the poor, creating a refuge from poverty utilizing leisure and educational programming. Addams and Starr wanted a place where people could go to escape poverty even if only temporarily. At Hull House, children and adults learned pottery, dance, photography, and participated in special events and attended concerts. It was also important to the founders that participants, primarily women, learned new skills that would be marketable in the workplace. Hull House became a model for social work and outreach that has been replicated across the United States and around the world.

Continued Perspectives of Leisure

The historical influences of leisure have affected our current views of leisure and the ways we consider leisure in society. The key point to remember is that leisure has a close connection to education, especially adult education, in changing behaviors and advancing the needs of society. This section describes views of leisure as time, activity, or state of mind. These descriptions suggest a hybrid of perspectives that indicate the important personal and social impact of leisure, especially in our ongoing discussion about adult education, lifelong learning, and learning cities.

Leisure as Time. Many people equate leisure with a specific period of time. It is typically related to discretionary time, or the time that remains when free from work and after accomplishing daily responsibilities or necessary commitments related to work and family (Rapoport & Rapoport, 1975; Stokowski, 1994). Therefore, it is reasonable to suggest that if leisure time is the time left over after the important obligations, then leisure time appears by default to be valued as less important. As such, living one's life has become a matter of prioritizing the use of time (Russell, 2009, 2013). In comparison to work time, it becomes easy to see why leisure time mistakenly takes on a lower priority and significance. What many people may not understand, however, is that by placing leisure time in higher regard, one may become even more productive at work and in performing other life obligations.

Leisure as Activity. Viewing leisure as activity describes the outward expressions freely chosen and self-determined (Kelly, 2012). Expressions such as "I am a karaoke singer," "I am a flag-football player," and "I am a cloud gazer" suggest freely chosen activities by individuals defining such activities as leisure performed in their discretionary time. However, if we delve deeper, these "I am" statements are powerful indicators of the development of identity. Leisure activities are instrumental for participants in the psychological process of self-development and the accompanying esteem that is associated with a strong sense of self. Therefore, leisure as an activity can be effective in assisting individuals to learn who they are in the context of their communities and the wider world around them, making leisure activities much more important than simply something one does in his or her spare time. When used effectively, leisure as activities can be an essential means of learning and enriching human development.

Leisure as State of Mind. Whereas leisure as time or as activity can be measured or described, leisure as a state of mind is more subjective, elusive, and difficult to quantify (Russell, 2009, 2013; Stokowski, 1994). Leisure as a state of mind is connected to feelings or attitudes of fulfillment, also freedom from obligations and constraints. As such, leisure can take on subjective, mental, emotional, psychological, and spiritual qualities (Kerr, 1962; Neulinger, 1981; Pieper, 1952; Stokowski, 1994). A theologian may refer to leisure as a connection to a supreme being. A psychologist may refer to self-actualization, or an environmentalist may connect leisure to nature. Irrespective of the discipline, leisure as a state of mind can connect with many values and beliefs in living an authentic life and becoming fully human. It is being human when paying attention to larger ideals, connecting to a universal energy, even experiencing the simple joy of being alive in knowing exactly what it feels like to be truly happy: to live and serve for truth and humanity.

New Directions for Adult and Continuing Education • DOI: 10.1002/ace

The results of leisure being related to time, activity, or status invite other values and perspectives. Thus, it is important to note that leisure is not solely an individual endeavor, but a social experience. Leisure has been described as a symbol of social status, yet leisure also has a social agency for the future in "transforming human beings" (Godbey, 2003). Such a future, as Godbey envisions, will have to do with increasing our quality of life and living healthier lives; "[w]hile humans have devoted centuries to changing the world, the next century will be devoted more to changing ourselves" (p. 383).

With the help of adult and continuing education, we believe that leisure can be the agent for social change through active human participation in developing *true* learning cities. The potential of social agency in the practice of leisure requires a "leisure education" (Verduin & McEwen, 1984) that expands our social networks for the purposes of improving individuals and rebuilding communities. In simple terms, learning cities can be measured by the number of social networks they create.

Developing Social Networks Through Leisure Education

"Network analysis is a style of social science research that focuses on people's social networks as a means toward understanding their behavior" (Fischer, 1977, p. 63). The primary focus of network analysis is on the interpersonal relationships of an individual and his or her various connections to community. This type of analysis differs from other social science approaches that concentrate on the individual and various institutions. With network analysis, researchers are focused on ties (the ways two social actors are involved with each other) and links (the total set of relations between any two social actors). When conducting a network study, a researcher must specify which links they are interested in for any given network analysis, because everyone is ultimately related to everyone else, either directly or indirectly. By utilizing the network analysis process, the behaviors of individuals within a learning city can be better understood, including the motivations and meanings surrounding their leisure participation and why and how they learn.

Various sociologists have made reference to the decline of the community in the United States. In fact, many authors contend that the concept of community no longer exists, particularly as it relates to the urban community. As cited in Wireman (1984), Tonnies's (1887) term *Gesellschaft* represents urban, capitalistic, industrial society where individuals relate only in contractual relationships for specific and limited purposes, primarily to further their individual economic goals. However, contemporary scholars are replacing the traditional notions of the American community with modern views on human interaction. The nature of American communities has changed, but community-sited relationships are still very much a force in daily human interaction; they must be given serious consideration in various contexts of social interaction and the development of learning cities, particularly using recreation and leisure (as a major vehicle for community learning).

Further, it is expected that learning cities would develop these networks because networks have endured the large-scale social transformations of urbanization, industrialization, bureaucratization, technological change, capitalism, and socialism (Wellman & Wortley, 1989). Individuals are linked to their communities primarily through relations with other individuals, such as relatives, friends, coworkers, and acquaintances. Each individual is the center of a web of social bonds that radiates outward from the individual to people who are known both intimately and casually, and to the wider society (Fischer, 1977). Our relationships become our personal social networks. Researchers (Fischer, 1977; Wellman & Wortley, 1989; Wireman, 1984) have found that Americans use social networks to gain support, establish group norms and values, develop knowledge, and maintain a modified version of community in spite of the changes in American social and economic culture.

Social networks also provide outlets for communication, leisure, and recreation. According to Wellman and Wortley (1989), this support is provided in four major dimensions: emotional aid, information/knowledge, companionship, and financial aid. These four dimensions are frequently used to study the depth of an individual's support system and are the foundation of network analysis. Community network ties with friends and relatives are a principal way by which people obtain supportive resources (Wellman & Wortley, 1989). Those relationships supply much of the social capital that people use to deal with daily life, seize opportunities, and reduce uncertainties (Coleman, 1988; DiMaggio & Mohr, 1985; Kadushin, 1972). They underpin the informal economic and social arrangements often crucial for a household's survival, expansion, and reproduction (Sik, 1978). Usually operating in ways that transcend narrow reciprocity, they are both a product and a cause of the roles that people play (Leifer, 1988). Social networks are critical for individuals and families, being the fundamental component of growing healthy communities and ensuring the ongoing success of the learning cities concept. Given that learning is often a communal process, viewing learning cities through the leisure lens of social networks will prove to be critical in establishing powerful learning cities across America. This process may in fact start a movement in leisure education that improves the quality of life and lifelong learning for all adults.

Final Words

Those in the leisure discipline have long understood that leisure is essential to the health and vitality of communities here in the United States and around the world. Additionally, leisure services comprise one of the largest and fastest growing industries in the world, whether measured in dollars spent, persons served, hours of time devoted, or resources used. The education of leisure is a broad discipline, combining diverse fields of study and professional practice

(Verduin & McEwen, 1984). A more comprehensive leisure education through lifelong learning, we believe, will transform individuals, thus starting the process of fully "humanizing" learning cities.

References

Bayley, R., Baynes, M., & Kendall, T. (2004). *About Nubia*. Retrieved from http://www .nubia.org/

Coleman, J. S. (1988). Social capital in the creation of human capital. *American Journal of Sociology, 94*, 95–120.

DiMaggio, P., & Mohr, J. (1985). Cultural capital, educational attainment, and marital selection. *American Journal of Sociology, 90*(6), 1231–1261.

Dumazedier, J. (1974). *Sociology of leisure* (M. A. McKenzie, Trans.). Philadelphia, PA: Elsevier.

Fife, S. (2012). *The roman domus*. Retrieved from http://www.ancient.eu/article/77/

Fischer, C. (1977). *Network and places: Social relations in the urban setting*. New York, NY: The Free Press.

Godbey, G. (2003). *Leisure in your life: An exploration*. State College, PA: Venture Publishing.

Ibrahim, H. (1991). *Leisure and society: A comparative approach*. Dubuque, IA: Wm. C. Brown.

Kadushin, A. (1972). The racial factor in the interview. *Social Work, 17*(3), 88–98.

Kaplan, M. (1960). *Leisure in America: A social inquiry*. New York, NY: Wiley.

Kaplan, M. (1975). *Leisure: Theory and policy*. New York, NY: Wiley.

Kelly, J. R. (2012). *Leisure* (4th ed.). Urbana, IL: Sagamore Publishing.

Kerr, W. (1962). *The decline of pleasure*. New York, NY: Simon & Schuster.

Kraus, R. (1971). *Recreation and leisure in modern society*. New York, NY: Meredith Corporation.

Kraus, R. (1994). *Leisure in a changing America: Multicultural perspectives*. Needham Heights, MA: Macmillan College Publishing.

Kraus, R. (2000). *Leisure in a changing America: Trends and issues for the twenty-first century* (2nd ed.). Upper Saddle River, NJ: Benjamin Cummings Pearson Education.

Leifer, E. M. (1988). Interaction preludes to role setting: Exploratory local action. *American Sociological Review, 53*, 865–878.

McBride, P. (1989). Jane Addams. In H. Ibrahim (Ed.), *Pioneers in leisure and recreation* (pp. 35–37). Reston, VA: American Alliance for Health, Physical Education, Recreation and Dance.

Neulinger, J. (1981). *The psychology of leisure*. Springfield, IL: Charles C. Thomas.

Pieper, J. (1952). *Leisure: The basis of culture* (A. Dru, Trans.). New York, NY: Pantheon Books.

Rapoport, R., & Rapoport, R. N. (1975). *Leisure and the family life cycle*. Boston, MA: Routledge & Kegan Paul.

Russell, B. (1935/1960). *In praise of idleness*. London, UK: George Allen & Unwin.

Russell, R. V. (2009). *Pastimes: The context of contemporary leisure* (4th ed.). Urbana, IL: Sagamore Publishing.

Russell, R. V. (2013). *Pastimes: The context of contemporary leisure* (5th ed.). Urbana, IL: Sagamore Publishing.

Sharma, P. (1990). *Sociology of leisure: Themes and perspectives*. New Delhi, India: Bahri Publications.

Sik, H. N. (1978). Minimal social categorization, political categorization, and power change. *Human Relations, 31*(9), 765–779.

Stokowski, P. A. (1994). *Leisure in society: A network structural perspective*. New York, NY: Villiers.

Sylvester, C. (1999). The classical idea of leisure: Cultural ideal or class prejudice? *Leisure Sciences, 12*, 3–16.

Tregear, M. (1985). *Chinese art*. New York, NY: Thames and Hudson.

Veblen, T. (1899). *The theory of the leisure class*. New York, NY: Macmillan.

Verduin, J. R., & McEwen, D. N. (1984). *Adults and their leisure: The need for lifelong learning*. Springfield, IL: Charles C. Thomas.

Wellman, B., & Wortley, S. (1989). Brothers' keepers: Situating kinship relations in broader networks of social support. *Sociological Perspectives, 32*(3), 273–306.

Wireman, P. (1984). *Urban neighborhoods, networks, and families: New forms for old values*. Lexington, KY: Lexington Books.

DAN K. HIBBLER *is an associate professor and associate dean at DePaul University– School for New Learning.*

LEODIS SCOTT *is a cofounder and research scholar at LearnLong Institute for Education and Learning Research, and lecturer in adult learning philosophy and practice at DePaul University–School for New Learning and Columbia University–Teachers College.*

7

This chapter features a conceptual framework that considers the practical characteristics of learning cities, pointing to the field of adult and continuing education to lead a movement for the purposes of education, learning, and engagement for all.

Learning Cities for All: Directions to a New Adult Education and Learning Movement

Leodis Scott

Previous chapters of this volume describe some necessary aspects for experiencing genuine learning cities. These aspects include developing communities, transforming organizations, and changing systems that redefine our public libraries, leisure, health, and well-being. As such, learning cities must have a goal of renewing their populations for serving education and learning for all. In learning cities, the adult learner population is of great importance in becoming the existing leaders for improving our quality of life.

This chapter places these aspects into a conceptual framework that points to a new direction for the adult and continuing education field. Although this volume discusses learning cities from an American perspective, its fundamental ideas may serve other countries and societies. Moreover, this chapter provides an additional description of learning cities along with thoughts about the philosophy, profession, and practice of adult learning. Finally, the more ambitious aim is to push forward a new movement: a movement changing outdated education and learning across every sector of society.

Description of Learning Cities and Their Citizenship

So far, multiple authors in this volume have discussed some descriptions of learning cities. These varied interpretations along with other descriptions about learning cities in Africa, Asia, Europe, and other societies enhance these views. It appears that a common theme among these views and interpretations about learning cities is the ongoing pursuit to motivate people to consider and serve more than their individual self. Thus, in my mind, learning cities can be literally described as *civitas cognitionis* (citizenship of learning), which is an imagined Latin phrase that captures the idea of the city representing a community coming together, as fellow learners, getting to know each other, and

NEW DIRECTIONS FOR ADULT AND CONTINUING EDUCATION, no. 145, Spring 2015 © 2015 Wiley Periodicals, Inc.
Published online in Wiley Online Library (wileyonlinelibrary.com) • DOI: 10.1002/ace.20125

becoming acquainted with their surroundings through reciprocal engagement (Scott, 2014) to their metropolitan city. The learning that takes place is not a luxury or optional, but rather essentially required to develop the educational enterprise that must address the issues and concerns of all citizens.

Recent developments about cities and urban planning confirm the immense potential of education and learning (Batty, 2013; Ehrenhalt, 2012; Florida, 2008; Gallagher, 2013), which in turn confirms the Faure Report (Faure et al., 1972) vision of the city that takes advantage of its multiple structures, networks, and exchanges. For example, Batty (2013) looks into the science of how cities can function as systems of networks. Gallagher (2013) pronounces the end of the suburbs and a return to the metropolitan areas that no longer will pursue the traditional American dream of a house, lawn, and picket fence, but rather multiple American dreams for the complex needs of diverse Americans. In addition, Richard Florida (2008) explores a creative economy and class, where the place one lives will affect educational opportunities that bear on one's success and happiness. Likewise, Ehrenhalt (2012) sees an American "demographic inversion" of cities and suburbs that will depend on the coming generation of adults. These accounts of the future of cities and their demographics are subjects important not only for urban planning or economics, but also for the field of adult and continuing education.

These kinds of traditional descriptions of a city strictly view metropolitan areas as "urban" that makes a needless distinction between rural areas, towns, and villages based on its larger population, local incorporation, and government municipality. Yet similarly, as with American land-grant institutions that serve the counties and parishes of the states and territories, learning cities could include both urban and rural communities expanding to regions that share knowledge, experience, and ideas in the broader citizenship of learning. Surely identifying learning cities by metropolitan areas, such as Chicago or New York, is a good way to start, but ultimately, the expansion of learning cities and the enterprise of education and learning must move across these municipal boundaries.

Describing learning cities as the citizenship of learning calls attention to the adult learner population within urban and rural areas. Irrespective of the geographic area, adult learners and their communities are involved in complex issues that need attention. The field of adult and continuing education can facilitate these complex issues within a learning cities framework, thus addressing the needs of the entire society.

Lessons Learned From Previous Chapters

The reality of learning cities cannot be actualized without considering the points made by authors of previous chapters in this volume. Their contributions offer valuable lessons for scholars, researchers, professionals, and practitioners of adult and continuing education. One of the key lessons learned begins with managing expectations, the contributing role of this final chapter.

As in many concluding chapters, once readers have become interested, there is a quick response to get the readers to do something immediate to get involved. In the same way, this chapter encourages involvement, but after the immediate enthusiasm subsides. Building learning cities will require sustained energy beyond the initial excitement. The talk of learning cities may be a thrilling topic, but our responses will be shortsighted if we do not find long-term solutions to the existing problems where we live.

This chapter encourages deliberative and sustained participation that steadily improves the lifelong development of communities. Forming local groups to discover real problems and finding practical solutions by using critical thinking skills for sustainable change may not be as thrilling decades from now, but will be essential in creating the learning cities that these chapter authors want to see.

As such, when you go back and read each of these chapters, curb your enthusiasm for immediate action into attentive endurance for seeing how all of us can transform the adult and continuing education field. The leadership required to construct learning cities must start from within and expand across disciplines. By teaming together, we can tackle the larger problems that cities face and that no one person can solve (such as crime, unemployment, violence, disease, and literacy). Many of the ideas expressed in this volume may seem lofty or impossible through the eyes of one individual, but likewise feel attainable through the combination of insights from a community of individuals, and even possible through the vision of an entire city and society of communities.

Addressing Both Education and Learning. All the previous chapters deal with the combination of both education and learning that merge into unique ways for describing learning cities. Watson and Tiu Wu (Chapter 1) bring back the dream of a learning society by making the distinctions between lifelong education and lifelong learning, and the scholarly practices of learning communities. The term learning cities is not original, but rather the newest installment in providing education and learning to the widest population of learners.

Many in the adult and continuing field are familiar with other related terms, such as organizational learning, which Yorks and Barto (Chapter 3) describe. Their chapter conceptualizes learning cities as a learning organization, since learning organizations are guided by principles and strategies. What these principles and strategies may consist of with examples are addressed in the other chapters.

Fitzgerald and Zientek (Chapter 2) suggest systems for decision making from the literature on engagement scholarship for higher education that includes civic, public, and community engagement along with service learning. In the context of learning cities, creating systems of engaged scholarship can fully establish community-based, participatory action research that informs its own society. Research projects would start from the ground up based on the real, nonspeculative issues of the community.

Such was the case in America regarding the history of public libraries, land-grant institutions, and cooperative extension programs that Peich and Fletcher (Chapter 4) explain. These authors describe how libraries were established to serve the adult learning community to help in their work, trade, and vocation. This chapter also provides existing examples of how governments and municipalities have played a direct role in the education and learning of their citizens by allocating public land and resources.

Howard, Howard, and Dotson (Chapter 5) place the concern for public health and education in the forefront of any description of learning cities. Their chapter offers components for consideration with implications to learning cities that include infrastructure, finance, and human resources. Placing public health into the context of learning cities also signals a new quality of life, education, and learning. Viewing learning cities from a historical, theoretical, and governmental lens suggests the broader principles and strategies by systems and organizations.

The chapter I coauthored with Hibbler (Chapter 6) advanced the disregarded role of leisure in partnering with adult education for the future construction of learning cities. In many ways, the Hibbler and Scott chapter shifts the focus from systems, institutions, and organizations to the sole learner, who must develop as an individual to become an active participant in the education and learning of others. Leisure invites a different way to see the quality and fulfillment of life: not just through the traditional lens of work, but rather through a comprehensive view of personal and social education transforming humanity. In the idea of learning cities, when it comes to leisure and work, economics is not the only aspect, but other social aspects must be nurtured.

Lastly, this final chapter contributes alongside the previous chapters in providing the mindset for constructing learning cities. Here is where the adult and continuing education field, with its overall theories and practices, can help in describing this outlook. To start, the actual profession, philosophy, and practice of adult learning can aid in adult and continuing education taking the lead.

Profession, Philosophy, and Practice of Adult Learning

In a seminal issue for *New Directions for Adult and Continuing Education*, Merriam (2001) offered a new update on adult learning theory that reconfirmed the continuing knowledge building of andragogy and self-directed learning. According to Merriam, andragogy and self-directed learning are the first two attempts to define adult learning as a unique field of practice. The "pillars" of andragogy and self-directed learning "will continue to engender debate, discussion, and research ... [that] enrich our understanding of adult learning" (Merriam, 2001, p. 11).

Many thinkers have contributed to the Knowlesian assumptions of andragogy and the adult characteristics of self-directed learning (Merriam, Caffarella, & Baumgartner, 2007). Yet criticisms that discuss the philosophical influence of humanistic psychology upon andragogy and self-directed learning require some deference, especially in the context of considering adult learning for the development of learning cities. Elias and Merriam (2005) explain the philosophical foundations of adult education and assess how the principles of humanism have affected all levels of education in the United States. With principles featuring the student in the center of the learning process, placing teachers as facilitators, and viewing learning as a highly personal endeavor, Elias and Merriam acknowledge the "strong hold" that the humanistic approach has on the philosophy of adult education, such that humanism "corresponds closely to the social and cultural values of contemporary America" (p. 145).

However, among the several philosophies described, Elias and Merriam (2005) position the promise of "analytic philosophy" as a central foundation for adult and continuing education. Embracing analytic philosophy could move adult and continuing educators beyond concepts and linguistic analyses to reconstruct the "educational enterprise in its full dimension ... [which] may well provide the strongest philosophical basis for contemporary philosophy of adult education" (p. 215). Although reconstructing learning cities as educational enterprises may be the right opportunity for the analytic philosophy of adult education, our field still has some unfinished business in reconciling its concepts and theories. This chapter calls attention to four specific theories of adult learning and education, namely lifelong learning, lifelong education, experiential education, and experiential learning (Scott, 2014). The analytic philosophical foundation can help further distinguish such theories and also help to reconcile historical differences between adult education and vocational training.

Reconciling the Roles of Adult and Continuing Education. One of the major takeaways from this chapter is to expand the scope of the adult education field to include diverse actions for broader education and learning in society. It comes with a vision of education and learning for all, existing in the common places and spaces of everyday living and human experience (Chen, Orum, & Paulsen, 2013).

Despite an all-inclusive view of the adult and continuing education field, it must at the same time reconcile decades of divisions with other areas, namely vocational education and corporate training. Eduard Lindeman (1926), a significant leader in our field, signaled this division when he inferred that adult education begins where "vocational education leaves off." Lindeman's conception of education was life-centered spanning a lifetime, and he called for a new kind of education with the assumption that "education is life" and not preparation for life, where learning is the whole of life and education has no ending (pp. 6–7). However, this view had also relegated traditional schooling and vocational training into a discounted category of education. A Lindeman biographer, David W. Stewart (1987), points out that "Lindeman must assume some of the blame for the continuing stepchild relationship of vocational education within the adult education family" (p. 105). Lindeman's articulation of education having no ending can arguably also have no divisions, thus expanding adult education to include all other concepts and practices.

Expanding Concepts of Adult Education and Learning. Although andragogy and self-directed learning have anchored much scholarship within the field, arguably the concept of lifelong learning has provided the widest opportunities to connect to other disciplines and levels of education. In America and Europe, numerous concepts of education such as permanent, recurrent, community, and lifelong have been largely morphed into concepts of lifelong learning and adult learning (Jarvis, 1995; Merriam et al., 2007). The lifelong learning concept supports the American emphasis on individual personal development and self-direction, but at the expense of ignoring the societal responsibility to provide education to its citizens (which is implied in the alternative *lifelong education*).

The dominance of lifelong learning has blurred the lines between education and learning (as distinctive domains; Thomas, 1991), both serving the person and the community, the individual and the society, the citizen and the city. For example, Merriam and Kee (2014) make the case for lifelong learning that promotes "community well-being" in older adults along with Brookfield (2012) considering the impact of lifelong learning on communities. These recent accounts provide additional opportunities to insert the adult and continuing education field into the affairs of the community. However, the theory and practice of lifelong learning must be combined with other theories such as lifelong education, experiential education, and experiential learning to provide a comprehensive approach to communities, and for the development of learning cities.

The concept of lifelong learning, set in isolation, suggests the discretionary choice to pursue learning as a luxury, without questioning the time, cost, and responsibility placed solely on the individual. It is clear that individuals pursuing lifelong learning would benefit as well as improve their society, yet alternatively, it is not as clear as to what the society, through its government, institutions, policies, and programs, would offer a community-of-individuals in return. Lifelong education, in contrast, calls for institutions and organizations to be also responsible for providing education for its people (Faure et al., 1972). Likewise, experiential education and experiential learning call for both institutions and individuals to bring a diversity of experiences (through engagement as a starting point) for the purposes of education and learning for all (Scott, 2014).

The adult and continuing education field can take a leadership role in facilitating the engagement and responsibilities between the community and individuals. However, the field is already at a disadvantage if lifelong learning is the sole option. Other theories, concepts, and philosophical discussions surrounding lifelong education, experiential education, as well as experiential learning could complement lifelong learning to expand the kinds of education and learning (for luxury and necessity) that develop individuals and

New Directions for Adult and Continuing Education • DOI: 10.1002/ace

communities. As such, creating a comprehensive framework of education and learning that serves the field in making stronger connections to other disciplines and professions is long overdue. The emergent focus of learning cities in America presents the right opportunity for the field to reveal its theories and concepts, research and practices on a comprehensive scale that will affect the quality of life for all.

During the discussion about learning cities, the speculative tone of this chapter may suggest a disregard of the practical aspects that relate to everyday practices and actions that people have done in alignment with this idea. This volume tries to offer particular examples, but still in the academic community, there remains a void for discussing the teaching, research, and service implications regarding the learning cities idea.

Teaching, Research, and Service of Learning Cities. Teaching, research, and service represent an adopted threefold mission of American higher education that dates back to the land-grant idea of U.S. institutions imparting knowledge to the people, especially for the farmer and his family (McDowell, 2001). These land-grant institutions still exist today either through cooperative extension, service-learning opportunities, and statewide collaboration efforts within each U.S. state and major territory.

The promise of offering education to the masses still resonates through values for access, inclusion, and diversity across American college campuses, public or private, land-grant or otherwise. Many commissions have attempted to renew the threefold mission that still captures this fundamental goal that promotes a mutual two-way relationship between college and community, reconciling old divisions of town versus gown, the ivory tower, and higher education for the privileged few.

The call for learning cities can be considered as another useful installment in the belief of education and learning for all. This call not only builds upon the land-grant idea, the traditional/renewed threefold mission, and the resistance against old divisions, but also calls for expanding views above higher education and beneath the feet of all people.

Learning cities are built by the changes of citizens demanding a continuance of education. Many learning cities in America may already exist, but will require a different way of identifying themselves. The number of schools, colleges, and universities in a metropolitan area may help, likewise the tally of libraries, parks and museums, sports and recreation areas. Yet it appears that the most accurate research will derive from the continual and lifelong assessments of citizens and their engaged experiences with education or learning, wherever it takes place.

Longworth (1999) believes that lifelong learning can provide the methodology, tools, and techniques for becoming learning cities. This chapter adds that both lifelong learning and lifelong education along with other theories and practices for adult learning, teaching, and research (namely, experiential learning and experiential education) can enhance the methodology. In order

Figure 7.1. Learning Cities for All Conceptual Map

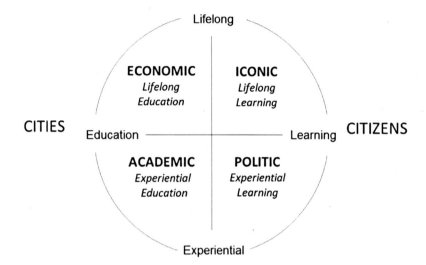

to aid in transferring the learning cities idea into daily practice, a conceptual map may help to illustrate the fullness of education and learning available for developing individuals and communities.

Learning Cities for All Conceptual Map

The learning cities map (Figure 7.1) is grounded on the analytic philosophical foundation of adult education that offers a conceptual analysis through clarifying issues of language (Elias & Merriam, 2005). Developed from previous discussions of adult learning theories and practices (Scott, 2014; Yorks & Scott, 2013), this conceptual map focuses on the essential aspects of the learning cities idea, especially in the context of the United States. In combination with our practical knowledge about adult learners, there are at least four characteristics that will affect the education and learning domains in metropolitan areas. The aspects namely are academic, economic, politic, and iconic in the philosophical analysis of cities and citizenship.

This figure represents four theories and practices of adult and continuing education by highlighting key aspects that will help advance learning cities in their engagement to citizens. Experiential education represents the academic aspects of education, while lifelong education represents the economic aspect. Experiential learning represents the politic aspect of learning, while lifelong learning represents the iconic. In short, these theories and aspects advance the villages framework (Weil & McGill, 1989) and social practices map (Usher, Bryant, & Johnston, 1997) that describe the overall experience, actions, and context of adults. These authors provide the basis for this conceptual framework that can be revised for the purposes of connecting learning cities to the theories and practices of adult and continuing education. The key take-away from this conceptual map is that education and learning represent two distinct domains that require interaction. It is a required interaction between systems of education (represented as cities) and individuals of learning (represented as citizens) to engage for the betterment of both. As such, this interaction introduces a new space, sight, and sound of engagement.

Future of Learning Cities: Engaging a New Movement

The central intent of this chapter and overall volume is to point the field of adult and continuing education in a new direction: a direction focusing on collaboration across academic spaces even within the traditional schools of elementary, secondary, and postsecondary education. It points toward a direction that sees education and learning as expansive and inclusive where every person, irrespective of age, gender, social, or cultural status, can belong to a community of educators and learners, wherever he or she lives; and can become a part of an ongoing legacy of engagement across generations. Such a grand intent cannot be housed in any one school, college, or university; it cannot be inserted into any one job, workplace, or company. Instead, it must reside in the homes and families, the communities and cities, the nations and societies where we all reside.

One of the hallmark tenets of adult and continuing education is the value of experience in educating learners. As many in the field know, experience through personal reflection and inquiry can become a source of new meaning and perspective that brings about new learning, knowledge, competence, and deep understanding. Still, if experience is expanded beyond individuals, and placed across the areas in which they live, then through social discussion and implementation, experience will feature a unique coexistence resulting from shared learning, vital education, and reciprocal engagement.

The idea of learning cities serves to spark the minds of citizens to start creating the spaces of education and learning for academic, economic, politic, and iconic purposes. The academic, economic, and politic purposes have been mostly described by many interested in the learning cities topic, but the iconic purpose needs more explanation. As such, the iconic aspect enhances the engagement between cities and citizens, and features the theory and practice of lifelong learning, not simply as unnoticed individual learning pursuits, but rather as widely recognizable expressions seen and shared by each person. The iconic aspect of this conceptual framework advertises the authentic "lifestyle" or brand of learning that inspires the individual, family, community, and city to continually change. This volume hopefully aims to advance an overall conceptual framework for further research practice and discussion.

The focus on cities and metropolitan areas (as expanded places for education and learning) comes with great promise. It is a promise that may restore many cities in education—academic reform or financial–economic decline with no hope of prosperity. It may call for the community to recommit to the politic well-being for all its people in hopes of living better. It could also demand a metropolitan focus for the cosmopolitan, iconic spirit of our global world. All of these happenings may occur from a simple shift in thinking about one another, educating each other about what it means to be human, and learning together on how we serve humanity.

But semantic language and phrasing that describe cities as "learning" require unique actions. It requires starting a movement—a movement not too different from other movements in America, where there is a long, overdue need to address problems. Some of the problems that this movement must address are misguided education, malnourished learning, and segregated disengagement across systems, communities, and neighborhoods. It is miseducation if the system has given credentials at a cost, without assurance of it being applicable and employable. It is mal-learning if the community has not inspired opportunities to create businesses, or other communities, organizations, and municipalities for the continued betterment and vitality of its members. Lastly, it is segregated disengagement when one neighbor is prosperous without fellow neighbors knowing how to reach for the same prosperity.

In short, the new space, sight, and sound of engagement advance all others by increasing our social harmony. As the space and sight of engagement expand, the sound is also a body of water, being flexible, adaptable, nourishing, and replenishing. One of the core principles of this new engagement is that we are all educators and learners, meaning that we not only can teach and learn from each other, but we have a duty as citizens of a community, city, even country to do so.

Becoming Facilitators of Learning Cities

What we all can do, especially practitioners and scholars in the field of adult and continuing education, is become the facilitators of learning cities, bringing all sectors together for the purpose of improving our lives. But in order for those to serve in this capacity, the field itself must reconcile age-old divisions between elementary, secondary, and traditional postsecondary education. It must heal the wounds of distinguishing itself from vocational training and corporate instruction. While it is true to suggest that the real classroom for the adult exists in the communities and cities where adults live, work, and play, it must nurture its relationships within educational organizations and systems to reach the most people possible (both children and adults).

Our field must be prepared to work alongside other disciplines to provide a link for interdisciplinary collaboration, service learning, and community leadership. The authors of this volume make an essential point in the idea of learning cities: the sole power and ability of citizens to construct their own cities appropriate to their needs. This power is based on thinking of education as developing lifelong leaders and discovering learning as practicing experiential solutions to the needs, problems, and opportunities of the community. The field through its theories and practices has long since been prepared to guide fellow citizens in becoming both educators and learners, scholars and practitioners, volunteers and friends.

At the same time, this volume challenges our field to include all levels of education and learning with comprehensive transformation. Basically, learning cities reflect their citizens' quality of life, insofar as an uneducated, unhealthy, unemployed, and uninspired citizenry can never become a learning city, irrespective of how many philosophies, policies, or proclamations are handed-down. Our current century must confront the realities that face metropolitan areas. This volume intended to illustrate present and future examples of how learning cities can function and how everyone, especially adults, can actively participate.

References

Batty, M. (2013). *The new science of cities*. Cambridge, MA: MIT Press.

Brookfield, S. (2012). The impact of lifelong learning on communities. In D. N. Aspin, J. Chapman, K. Evans, & R. Bagnall (Eds.), *Second international handbook of lifelong learning* (part 2, pp. 875–886). New York, NY: Springer.

Chen, X., Orum, A. M., & Paulsen, K. E. (2013). *Introduction to cities: How place and space shape human experience*. West Sussex, UK: Wiley-Blackwell.

Ehrenhalt, A. (2012). *The great inversion and the future of the American city*. New York, NY: Alfred A. Knopf.

Elias, J. L., & Merriam, S. B. (2005). *Philosophical foundations of adult education* (3rd ed.). Malabar, FL: Kreiger.

Faure, E., Herrera, F., Kaddoura, A., Lopes, H., Petrovsky, A., Rahnema, M., & Ward, F. R. (1972). *Learning to be: The world of education today and tomorrow* (Faure Report). Paris, France: UNESCO.

Florida, R. (2008). *Who's your city? How the creative economy is making where to live the most important decision of your life*. New York, NY: Perseus.

Gallagher, L. (2013). *The end of the suburbs: Where the American Dream is moving*. New York, NY: Penguin.

Jarvis, P. (1995). *Adult and continuing education: Theory and practice* (2nd ed.). New York, NY: Routledge.

Lindeman, E. C. (1926). *The meaning of adult education*. New York, NY: New Public.

Longworth, N. (1999). *Making lifelong learning work: Learning cities for a learning century*. Sterling, VA: Kogan Page.

McDowell, G. R. (2001). *Land-grant universities and extension into the 21st century: Renegotiating or abandoning a social contract*. Ames, IA: Iowa State University Press.

Merriam, S. B. (2001). Andragogy and self-directed learning: Pillars of adult learning theory. In S. B. Merriam (Ed.), *New Directions for Adult and Continuing Education: No. 89. The new update on adult learning theory* (pp. 3–13). San Francisco, CA: Jossey-Bass.

Merriam, S. B., Caffarella, R. S., & Baumgartner, L. M. (2007). *Learning in adulthood: A comprehensive guide*. San Francisco, CA: Jossey-Bass.

Merriam, S. B., & Kee, Y. (2014). Promoting community wellbeing: The case for lifelong learning for older adults. *Adult Education Quarterly, 64*(2), 128–144.

Scott, L. (2014). Experience of engagement as starting point. In C. J. Boden-McGill & K. P. King (Eds.), *Developing and sustaining adult learners* (pp. 17–34). Charlotte, NC: Information Age.

Stewart, D. (1987). *Adult learning in America: Eduard Lindeman and his agenda for lifelong education*. Malabar, FL: Kreiger.

Thomas, A. M. (1991). *Beyond education: A new perspective on society's management of learning*. San Francisco, CA: Jossey-Bass.

Usher, R., Bryant, I., & Johnston, R. (1997). *Adult education and the postmodern challenge: Learning beyond the limits*. New York, NY: Routledge.

Weil, S. W., & McGill, I. (1989). A framework for making sense of experiential learning. In S. Weil & I. McGill (Eds.), *Making sense of experiential learning: Diversity in theory and practice* (pp. 3–24). Philadelphia, PA: Society for Research into Higher Education & Open University Press.

Yorks, L., & Scott, L. (2013). Lifelong tools for the learner, educator, and worker. In V. C. X. Wang (Ed.), *Handbook of research on technologies for improving the 21st century workforce: Tools for lifelong learning* (pp. 42–55). doi:10.4018/978-1-4666-2181-7.ch004

LEODIS SCOTT is a cofounder and research scholar at LearnLong Institute for Education and Learning Research, and lecturer in adult learning philosophy and practice at DePaul University–School for New Learning and Columbia University–Teachers College.

INDEX

Aaronson, D., 67, 68
Abbott vs. Burke, 65
Abel, A., 37, 42
Ackoff, R. L., 24, 31
Adams, H. B., 46, 48
Adult education: concepts of, 88–89; and learning cities, 12–13; profession, philosophy, and practice of, 86–89; at public libraries, 47–50; roles of, 87–88
Alegre, J., 38
Alexander, D., 14, 15
Alpaslan, C. M., 24, 31
American Library Association (ALA), 48
Arceo, F. D. B., 22
Argyris, C., 36

Baker, G., 67
Bakker, M., 15
Barnes-Najor, J. V., 27
Barto, J., 2, 35, 44
Batty, M., 84
Baumann, H., 38
Baumgartner, L. M., 86
Bayley, R., 74
Baynes, M., 74
Bechara, J. P., 23, 31
Belden, G., 67
Berne, R., 58, 61
Bitterman, J., 13
Bliss, R. K., 49
Bobinski, G. S., 47
Book, P., 26
Boshier, R., 6, 7, 8
Boud, D., 36
Boyer, E. L., 3, 28
Boyte, H., 28, 30
Brookfield, S., 88
Brown, L. D., 40
Brown, R. E., 27
Brownson, R. C., 59
Brukardt, M. J., 26
Brunner, H. S., 46
Bruns, K. S., 26
Bryan, R. L., 59
Bryant, I., 90
Burtless, G., 67
Byun, J., 41

Caffarella, R. S., 86
Carmalt, J., 63
Carnegie Foundation, 47
Carroll, T. G., 68
Carter, B., 67
Cell, E., 36
Chen, X., 87
Chiva, R., 38
Christensen, C. M., 38
Cities and Regions in the New Learning Economy, 9
Clawson, M., 48
Clifford, G. J, 62
Cohn, D., 59
Coleman, J. S., 80
Community engagement scholarship (CES), 21–31; and learning cities/regions, 22–25; overview, 21–22; service learning, 28–30; university–community partnerships, 26
Coombs, W. T., 40
Cooper, D. D., 22
Cooper, R. A., 68
Cooperative Extension programs, 45–54
Crossing the Quality Chasm, 58, 67
Cutler, D. M., 61

Davis, K., 64
Dechant, K., 38, 39, 41
Delbanco, S., 67
DiBella, A. J., 38
DiMaggio, P., 80
Ditzion, S. H., 49
Doberneck, D. M., 27, 29
Dotson, E., 2, 57, 71
Dumazedier, J., 74

Eatman, T. K., 28
Education, and learning cities: business demanding reforms in, 66–67; components of, 60–68; cost and quality of, 64–65; financial resources, 63–66; health care, similarities with, 58–59; historical facts of, 61; human resources, 66–68; infrastructure, 61–63; management of, 62–63; organizational structure of, 65; outcomes of, 67;

overview, 57–58; perceived value of, 63–64; rural–urban issues in, 65–66; staff shortages, 67–68; theories of, 59–60; threat from international systems, 61–62
Ehrenhalt, A., 84
Elias, J. L., 87, 90
Escrigas, C., 28
EUROlocal, 9
European Lifelong Learning Initiative (ELLI), 9
Experiential education, 90
Experiential learning, 90

Faure, E., 3, 6, 84, 88
Fife, S., 75
Fillery-Travis, A., 36
Financial Industry Regulatory Authority (FINRA) Investor Education Foundation, 51–52
Fiol, M. C., 38
Fischer, C., 79, 80
Fisher, D., 40
Fitzgerald, H. E., 1, 21, 26, 27, 28, 33
Fletcher, C. N., 2, 45, 51, 55
Florida, R., 61, 84
Foster, E., 68
Fox, J., 40
Freire, P., 6, 30
Friedman, V. J., 37, 38, 39, 40
Furco, A., 26

Gallagher, L., 84
Galvin, R. S., 67
Garman, A. N., 62
Garrick J., 36
Gazley, B., 30
Gesellschaft, 79
Getzen, T., 68
Gilton, D. L., 48, 50
Glass, C. R., 28, 29
Godbey, G., 74, 79
Goettel, R., 26
Goldin, C., 66
Goleman, D., 40
Gordon, G. J., 57
Gould, J. M., 38
Graham, H. D., 58
Grandio, A., 38

Guagliardo, M. F., 66
Guthrie, J. W., 62

Haft, J., 26
Hall, B., 28
Hamilton, R., 8
Health care, and learning cities: business demanding reforms in, 66–67; components of, 60–68; cost and quality of, 64–65; education, similarities with, 58–59; financial resources, 63–66; health belief model, 60; historical facts of, 61; human resources, 66–68; infrastructure, 61–63; management of, 62–63; organizational structure of, 65; outcomes of, 67; overview, 57–58; perceived value of, 63–64; rural–urban issues in, 65–66; staff shortages, 67–68; theories of, 59–60; threat from international systems, 61–62
Heim, K. M., 47
Helliwell, J., 15, 16
Herrera, F., 3, 6, 84, 88
Hibbler, D. K., 2, 73, 82
Hightower, A., 64
Hill, L. H., 59, 60, 68
Hipp, K. K., 12
Holladay, S. J., 40
Holland, B., 26
Howard, D., 2, 57, 63, 71
Howard, J., 2, 57, 71
Howard, J. E., 65
Huffman, J. B., 12
Hughes, C., 13

IaLS. See Iowa Library Services (IaLS)
Ibrahim, H., 76
Illeris, K., 36
IMLS. See Institute of Museum and Library Services (IMLS)
In Praise of Idleness, 76
Institute of Museum and Library Services (IMLS), 50–52
In the Nation's Compelling Interest, 58–59
Iowa Library Services (IaLS), 45; partnership with ISUEO, 51–53
Iowa State University Extension and Outreach (ISUEO), 45, 49; partnership with IaLS, 51–53

Iqbal, M. J., 6, 7
ISUEO. *See* Iowa State University Extension and Outreach (ISUEO)

Jackson, S., 6
Jarvis, P., 5, 6, 7, 8, 36, 88
Johansson, F., 12
Johns, M. M., 68
Johnson, A. S., 47
Johnson, T. J., 62
Johnston, R., 90
Jordan, L., 8
Juceviciene, P., 5, 11

Kaddoura, A., 3, 6, 84, 88
Kadushin, A., 80
Kang, F., 14
Kaplan, M., 75, 77
Kasl, E., 36, 38, 39, 41
Kearns, P., 11, 12, 14, 26, 66
Kee, Y., 88
Kegan, R., 8
Kelly, J. R., 74, 78
Kendall, T., 74
Kerr, W., 78
Knowledge, Engagement & Higher Education: Contributing to Social Change, 28
Knowles, N. S., 49
Kraus, R., 74, 75, 77
Kreuter, M. W., 59

Land-grant universities, in 19th century, 46–47
Landry, C., 11
Laszlo, A., 11, 12
Laszlo, K., 11, 12
Lawler, P., 59
Layard, R., 14, 15, 16
Learned, W. S., 47, 48
Learning by organizations (LBO), 37–38
Learning cities, 5–17, 83–93; challenges and limitations of, 13–14; and citizenship, 83–84; conceptual map of, 90–91; evolution of, 5–11; facilitators of, 92–93; future of, 91–92; implications and actions for adult education, 12–13; milestones, 9–11; overview, 5; reconstruction of, 11–12; teaching, research, and service of, 89–90
Learning Cities 2020, 13

Learning Cities Audit Tool, 9
Learning Cities Networks, 13
Learning cities/regions (LCRs), 22–25
Learning in Local and Regional Authorities (LILARA) Project, 10
Learning in organizations (LIO), 37–38
Learning society, 6–9
Learning systems: expansion of, 41–42; organizational learning, 35–38; societal learning, 40–41; workplace learning, 35–37
Lee, R. E., 47, 48
Leifer, E. M., 80
Leigh, R. D., 49, 52
Leisure, 73–81; as activity, 78; birthplace of, 74; definition of, 73–74; historical influences of, 74–77; Industrial Revolution, influence of, 76–77; intellectual and physical nature of, 75; for life balance and lifelong learning, 76; overview, 73; for social control, 75–76; and social networks, development of, 79–80; as state of mind, 78–79; as time, 78; for wealthy social class, 76
Lifelong education, 6–9, 90
Lifelong learning, 6–9, 90; leisure for, 76; and lifelong engagement, 30
LILLIPUT Project, 10
Limerick Declaration, 10
Lindeman, E. C., 87
Lindorff, D., 65
Lipshitz, R., 37, 38, 39, 40
Littlepage, L., 30
Longworth, N., 3, 5, 8, 9, 10, 11, 26, 39, 41, 89
Lopes, H., 3, 6, 84, 88
Lupton, D., 15
Lyles, M. A., 38

Mackenbach, J., 15
Maki, P. L., 12
Malcolm, T., 13
Marmot, M., 15
Marsick, V. J., 13, 14, 36, 37, 38, 39, 41
Mayfield-Johnson, S., 59
McBride, P., 77
McCann, J., 65
McDowell, G. R., 46, 51, 89
McEwen, D. N., 73, 74, 79
McGill, I., 90

McGinnis, S., 59
McNall, M. A., 27
Meckel, K., 67, 68
Merriam, S. B., 86, 87, 88, 90
Mezirow, J., 22, 30, 36, 38
Milakovich, M. E., 57
Mills, G. E., 36
Milstein, A., 67
Missing Persons, 59
Mitroff, I. I., 24, 31
Mohr, J., 80
Monroe, M. E., 47
Montenegro, C., 60, 62
Moore, J., 59
Moyer, A., 60
Museums, Libraries and 21st Century Skills, 50
Myers, K. K., 37

Nam, T., 61
Nation at Risk, A, 67
National Resources Planning Board (NRPB), 48
Needleman, J., 65
Neulinger, J., 78
Nevis, E. C., 38
Nicolaides, A., 37
Nonaka, I., 23, 26
Norman, A. C., 47

Odendaal, N., 61
OECD. *See* Organization for Economic Co-operation and Development (OECD)
O'Neil, J., 14
Organizational learning, 35–38; key elements, 38; learning conditions, 39; learning modes, 38–39; mechanisms, 37–39
Organization for Economic Co-operation and Development (OECD), 7, 9–10, 22–23, 26, 62
Organization learning mechanism (OLM), 37–39
Orum, A. M., 87
Osborne, M., 5, 8, 9, 10, 11, 14, 26

Pace, R. W., 36
Paine, S. L., 62, 66
PALLACE Project, 10
Palmer, T., 65

Pardo, T. A., 61
Passell, J., 59
Passmore, J., 36
Patient Protection and Affordable Care Act, 68
Patrinos, H., 60, 62
Paulsen, K. E., 87
Peich, A., 2, 45, 51, 55
Percy, S. L., 26
Peters, S. J., 28
Petersen, A., 15
Petrovsky, A., 3, 6, 84, 88
Pieper, J., 78
Pikett, K., 27
Pinkham, D., 40
Pinzon, D. P., 22
Place and Social Capital and Learning (PASCAL), 10–11
Pleasant, A., 59
Popper, M., 37, 38, 39, 40
Post-War Standards for Public Libraries, 48
Pratt, A. C., 61
Program for International Student Assessment (PISA) tests, 62
Public libraries, 45–54; as centers for adult education, 47–50; ISUEO and IaLS partnership, 51–53; and land-grant universities, 46–47; overview, 45–46; partnership with Cooperative Extension, 50–53

Qualification Systems: Bridges to Lifelong Learning, 7

Rahnema, M., 3, 6, 84, 88
Rapoport, R. N., 78
Robinson vs. Cahill, 65
Rodin, K., 26
Rosenstock, I. M., 60
Ross-Lee, B., 68
Rothman, R., 65
Rowden, R., 36
Ruggles, R., 38
Russell, B., 76
Russell, L., 61, 76, 78
Russell, R. V., 74, 75
Ryu, K., 41

Sachs, J., 15, 16
Sachs, G., 16
Sadaghiani, K., 37

Sadtler, T. M., 38
Sanchez, J. G., 28
Schleicher, A., 62, 66
Schoen, C., 64
Schön, D. A., 36
Schweider, D., 50
Schweitzer, J. H., 29
Scott, L., 3, 4, 73, 82, 83, 84, 87, 88, 90, 94
Senge, P. M., 38
Sharma, P., 74
Sheldon, G. F., 68
Sik, H. N., 80
Simon, L. A. K., 26, 28
Smith, M. K., 6, 7
Smith, P. C., 26, 36
Societal learning, 40–41
Sohl, S. J., 60
Song, G., 14
Sonka, S. T., 26
Springer, N. C., 27
Stage, F. K., 22
Starr, P., 59
Stewart, D., 87
Stiefel, L., 58, 61
Stokowski, P. A., 74, 77, 78
Strategy for Kaunas as a Learning City, 11
Stremlkis, K., 64
Su, Y., 8
Sun, Q., 5, 8, 15
Swanson, L., 26
Sylvester, C., 75
Symonds, W. C., 65

Takeuchi, H., 23, 26
Taleb, N. N., 30
Tandon, R., 28
Theory of the Leisure Class, The, 76
Thomas, A. M., 88
To Err is Human, 67

Torbert, W. R., 40
Tregear, M., 76

Usher, R., 90

Van de Ven, A. H., 23, 31
van der Veen, R., 13
Veblen, T., 74, 76
Verduin, J. R., 73, 74, 79

Waddell, S. J., 40
Wain, K., 3
Walter, P., 59
Wang, A., 14
Ward, F. R., 3, 6, 84, 88
Watkins, K. E., 36, 37
Watson, C., 1, 5, 19
Weber, L., 42
Weil, S. W., 90
Weinrub, A., 59
Wellman, B., 80
Wells, R. S., 22
Whitcomb, M. E., 68
Wilkinson, R. G., 15, 27
Wireman, P., 79, 80
Wittrock, M. C., 38
Wood, P., 11
Workplace learning, 35–37
World Initiative on Lifelong Learning (WILL), 9
Wortley, S., 80
Wu, A. T., 1, 5, 19

Yang, J., 14, 26
Yorks, L., 2, 35, 36, 37, 39, 40, 42, 44, 90

Zadek, S., 40
Zaidi, S., 63
Zientek, R., 1–2, 21, 33
Zimpher, N., 26